Spanish
Beginner

Tony Buzan
with **Carmen García del Río**
& **Diego de Jesús Flores-Jaime**

HarperCollins Publishers
77-85 Fulham Palace Road
London W6 8JB
Great Britain

First edition 2009

Reprint 10 9 8 7 6 5 4 3 2 1 0

© HarperCollins Publishers 2009
Message from Tony © Tony Buzan 2008

ISBN 978-0-00-730342-7

www.collinslanguage.com

A catalogue record for this book is available
from the British Library

HarperCollins Publishers, 10 East 53rd Street,
New York, NY 10022

Collins Language Revolution Spanish –
Beginner
First US Edition 2009

ISBN 978-0-06-177436-2

Library of Congress Cataloging-in-Publication
Data has been applied for
www.harpercollins.com

Illustrations by Nina Chakrabarti & Hanna
Merlin
Typeset by Marc Marazzi & Joerg
Hartmannsgruber

Printed in China through Golden Cup Printing
Services

EDITORIAL DIRECTOR
Eva Martínez

SERIES EDITOR
Rob Scriven

Contents

A message from Tony Buzan

Your language learning adventure begins ...

Welcome to an entirely new, invigorating, exciting, and fun universe of language learning!

The journey you are now beginning will change your life; it will improve your ability to learn not only a language, but also *anything* else you wish to learn. The journey will open your mind and your body, will refresh your spirit, and will bring added richness and enjoyment to everything you do.

A huge number of exciting discoveries await you, including the fact that using your imagination and having fun will accelerate your language learning. That's right, **IMAGINATION** and **ASSOCIATION** are the Twin Pillars of your language learning: the more you can **imagine** the images of the words you are learning and the *pictures* that represent those words, the faster your language learning will be. The Twin Pillars of **Imagination** and **Association** guarantee that if you can find links between *anything* you know and the new words you are learning, you will learn faster *and* have more fun!

You will also discover that the dreaded "forgetting curve" can be turned, instead of the enemy it has always been, into one of your greatest companions on your language learning journey.

In addition you will be introduced to the fascinating revelation that your language learning is based just as much on your *vision* as on your hearing. This new awareness will enable you to take in new language learning information at a minimum of double the rate. Not only will you double your pleasure and double your fun, you will double, and more, the rate at which you accelerate your language learning.

Underlying all these new discoveries will be *the* language learning tool — the Mind Map®. I will show you how Mind Maps are the universal human language, and how applying them to acquiring any other national language makes learning much, much easier.

On the journey you will be aided by many support systems, including: an interactive, designed-especially-for-you website; new Mind Map® language learning software; and a phonetic system that will give you instant access to the language you are learning.

Through *Collins Language Revolution*, all the examples will be made relevant to your life, and will drench you in enjoyment and fun. And above all, remember, humor is a language. Speak it!

You are on your way!

How to use this book

Congratulations! You are on the way to experiencing the pleasures of speaking and understanding a new language — Spanish — in a way that is fun and easy.

This book is based on the following principles:

1. Association, Imagination, and Mind Mapping

We remember best when we can associate what we are learning with something we already know. In this book the Spanish words are divided into three categories, like the three colors of traffic lights.

These words are the same or nearly the same in English and in Spanish, even if there are some different uses for them.

Green
FOR GO AHEAD

Example: The Spanish word for *information* is información. Nearly all words that end in *-ion* in English are the same in Spanish. You can use words like this right from the beginning. You only need to practice the way they are pronounced in Spanish, which is sometimes very different from the English way. You will find plenty of help with this from the voices on the CDs and from the pronunciation guidance in the book, which shows how new words sound in Spanish alongside their Spanish spelling.

Just remember that in Spanish almost every letter in a word is pronounced, unlike in English and French, where there are lots of silent letters.

The good news is that literally thousands of words are either exactly the same or very similar in the two languages.

Yellow
FOR WAIT
AND THINK

These Spanish words may remind you of words in English that are not the same, but similar.

Example: The Spanish word for white is blanco, which looks and sounds like the English word *blank*. For yellow words, just slow down and think a little to find a link between the Spanish word and a word you know in English.

Red
FOR STOP, THINK,
MAKE A LINK

Stop and think! These words may have nothing in common with their English translation, but you can remember them by finding a funny, memorable association.

Play with the sound of the Spanish to find a word or phrase it resembles in English. The pronunciation of your association might be slightly off target, but the CDs and the pronunciation guidance will help you put it right. What's important is that it sticks in your head.

The association technique is a key feature of the course. It's more fun than learning by heart and much more efficient too. We're making languages easier by making those difficult foreign words sound quite familiar. Even if it seems stupid, try it and see if it helps you to remember. The trick is to let your mind create images as wild and vivid as in dreams. Imagined sounds, smells, and other sensations will link the memory to different parts of your brain, which will help you to remember the image and the Spanish word.

Example: The word for *belt* in Spanish is **cinturón**. To work well, the association technique needs a strong visualization. A way to remember this could be visualizing a Roman CENTURION in a film, wearing an enormous shiny *belt* — **cinturón** — ready to take his men into battle.

Now, without looking back, you should find it easy to remember the Spanish words for *information*, *white*, and *belt*. Try it!

Using Mind Maps: Why Mind Maps?

Mind Maps are simply one of the best thinking tools available. They are used widely throughout the course and you will master how to make and use them yourself. Making them is lots of fun, and they will help you visualize and retain new information. Remember that the best Mind Maps are the ones you draw yourself. You will add new branches for important words and create your own Mind Maps as you learn Spanish.

To make your own Mind Maps, take a blank piece of paper (the bigger the better) and some colored pens. Turn the page to landscape format, to make a wide rectangle.

In the middle draw an image of what your Mind Map is about: for example, if it's about food, draw something delicious.

Then draw branches coming out in all directions from your central image, one for each main group of words.

Connect second-level branches to the first, and third-level branches to those. Make your branches curves rather than straight lines and use colors and images throughout. In our example you could draw vegetables, meat, fruit, fish ... Then you can start adding the Spanish words for the food items you want to learn.

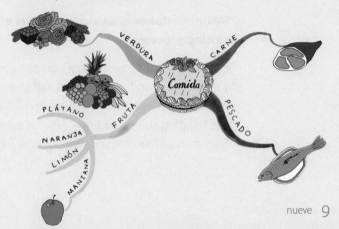

Making Mind Maps will help you to be more creative. Every branch you add strengthens the connections in your brain and helps to spark off new ideas. Review your Mind Maps regularly, not only just after studying a unit in the book but between your formal study sessions too. Whenever you come across a new word or expression that you think will be useful, add it to the appropriate Mind Map.

2. Body Language

Words aren't the only thing!

Only about 10% of communication is verbal. That's right, ten percent! Ninety percent of what we communicate is not what we say but the way that we say it, including our gestures and facial expressions. When words fail us — and they invariably will when we're speaking a foreign language — we will still be able to get our message across.

3. No Mistake, No Gain!

Making mistakes is an essential part of the learning process.

Don't be afraid to have a go. If you can get rid of your self-consciousness and simply go ahead and try out your new language, you will make rapid progress and maybe have a good laugh at the same time. Almost everyone who ever had the joy of learning a new language has a story about making a horrendous blunder — using the wrong word or mispronouncing it so badly it sounded like another, highly offensive, word!

4. Repeat and Succeed!

Repetition and memory go hand in hand.

In the process of learning a foreign language, first you will have to understand, then to learn, and finally you will have to remember what you have learned in order to be able to communicate. Revision is an essential part of the process.

To fix information in your long-term memory you should repeat it at fixed points, following this formula:

1st repetition: **an hour or so** after you first learn it
2nd repetition: **a day** after you first learn it
3rd repetition: **a week** after you first learn it
4th repetition: **a month** after you first learn it
5th repetition: **six months** after you first learn it

If you follow this winning formula you will permanently memorize what you want to learn — and even start to remember more, as your brain will be actively working with the new information it's storing and so will start to make new links between what it already knows.

5. Rest and Learn Best

Study breaks are essential to learning.

You will find it easier to retain information if you take regular breaks between study sessions. Ideally you should study for about 45 minutes, then break for five or ten minutes. While you relax, your brain will be busy sorting through and filing the information you have given it. When you return to your studies, your brain will feel refreshed and you will find it easier to concentrate.

Another advantage is that your brain remembers things more easily from the start and end of a study session than from the middle. With regular breaks, the middle of your study session is shorter and less information is at risk of being lost.

6. Your Personal Learning Style

Everyone has his or her own way of learning, and what works for one person may not work for another.

That's why we've put a questionnaire — Find Your Learning Style! — on our website (www.collinslanguage.com/revolution) to help you identify which learning techniques are best for you.

The three learning styles are **visual**, **auditory**, and **tactile**. Visual learners learn by looking at things, auditory learners learn best by listening, and tactile learners like to do something in order to absorb the information. Whichever style you prefer, you are likely to benefit from other learning techniques, too. Many people blend two or all three of the learning styles. We encourage you to use all of your brain while learning Spanish, and that means working on areas that are not necessarily your current strengths. Not only will you learn Spanish faster, but you will sharpen your brain for a whole host of other activities.

7. Using the book, the CDs and the website

Your course consists of this book and two CDs (CD1 and CD2), with online support and practice material.

The book is divided into practical units that will give you the vocabulary and expressions you need to communicate in Spanish, and it is accompanied by CD1. CD2 can be used independently from the book, which is great for when you are in the car, on public transportation or in the park.

Doing the practice exercises on the CDs is crucial if you want to make progress. Nobody ever learned to speak just by reading a book. The book will give you the words, sentences and strategies you need to learn, while the CDs will help you to speak and understand, to get your pronunciation right and to develop your ear for spoken Spanish.

It is a good idea to schedule some study time (a little every day is much better than several hours once a week) when you can sit down with the book and CD1 and put to use your three ways of learning: **visual** (Mind Maps, associations, imagination, and illustrations), **auditory** (listening and speaking practice), and **tactile** (writing things down, making flash cards and so on).

You can visit www.collinslanguage.com/revolution for lots of extra interactive exercises, to find out more about Mind Maps and to print or download interactive Mind Maps. You will be able to modify and expand all the Mind Maps in the book to help you test and reinforce your learning. First you will need to download and install the iMindMap™ software on your computer. The website also contains answers to the exercises in the book and transcripts for all the recordings.

In this course we've used a simple system to help you pronounce words and phrases. Use it for guidance, but always try to imitate the real sound of the Spanish that you hear on the CDs.

	sound	example	pronunciation
ca	ka	cama	**ka**-ma
co	ko	con	kon
cu	koo	documento	do-koo-**men**-to
ce	se	centro	**sen**-tro
ci	see	cinco	**sin**-co
ga	ga	garganta	gar-**gan**-ta
go	go	algo	**al**-go
gu	goo	segundo	se-**goon**-do
ge	khe	gente	**khen**-te
gi	khee	giro	**khee**-ro
j	kh	jueves	**khwe**-bes
ll	y	tortilla	tor-**tee**-ya
ñ	ny	señor	se-**nyor**
que	ke	queso	**ke**-so
qui	kee	aquí	a-**kee**
ua	wa	agua	**a**-gwa
ue	we	cuenta	**kwen**-ta
v	b	vino	**bee**-no
z	s	zapato	sa-**pa**-to

h is silent: **hora** (*o-ra*), **hola** (*o-la*).

r is rolled and **rr** even more so.

In Spanish, vowels (**a**, **e**, **i**, **o**, **u**) have only one sound. When you find two together, pronounce both of them in quick succession, as in **aceite** (*a-**sey**-te*).

Stress usually falls on the next-to-last syllable (**que**so, **jue**ves). If the word ends in a consonant other than **n** or **s**, it normally falls on the last syllable (se**ñor**). A written accent marks the stress in words that don't follow this pattern. We've shown the stressed syllable in bold (ja**món**, **lá**piz, te**lé**fono).

1

En el bar

By the end of this unit you will be able to:

- Greet people — say "good morning" and "goodbye"
- Buy drinks and snacks
- Say "please" and "thank you"
- Ask for the check
- Create your first Mind Map

Bebidas *(be-**bee**-das)*

Drinks

En el bar means *in the bar*. The word **bar** is the same in English and Spanish. Before learning how to ask for **bebidas** *drinks* and **botanas** *snacks* in a bar, let's start with some really easy Spanish words for drinks.

Green
FOR GO AHEAD

una Coca-Cola® *(**oo**-na **ko**-ka **ko**-la)* a Coke®

una botella *(**oo**-na bo-**te**-ya)* a bottle

un té *(oon te)* a tea

These green words are the same or nearly the same in English and Spanish (although the pronunciation is different), so they're easy to recognize. In this course you'll meet hundreds of Spanish words that are the same or nearly the same as their English equivalents. Try to visualize the "GREEN FOR GO AHEAD" traffic light when recalling these words.

The pronunciation guidance in brackets and the notes on page 15–16 will help you to say the Spanish words. Above all, though, listen carefully to the pronunciation on the CDs.

Now let's look at a few more words.

un café *(oon ka-**fe**)* a coffee

un vino *(oon **bee**-no)* a wine

un refresco *(oon re-**frais**-ko)* a soda

agua mineral *(**a**-gwa mee-ne-**ral**)* mineral water

por favor *(por fa-**bor**)* please

Yellow
FOR WAIT
AND THINK

 1

Listen to the green and yellow words on CD1 and practice saying them.

How to remember yellow words

Yellow words aren't as close as green words, but you'll probably find something that connects the English with the Spanish, and this will help you recall the Spanish word. For example, the Spanish word for *coffee* is **café**, which sounds just like "café," a place to go for a coffee. Imagine a yellow cup of lovely steaming coffee on a black and white table in a black and white café. Repeat the word three times and memorize the sound with this image.

The Spanish for *water* is **agua**. To remember this, think of "aquarium," a tank full of water, and change the pronunciation *(**a**-gwa)*.

Wine is **vino**: think of the English word "vine" and change it to **vino** (pronounced ***bee**-no*). Imagine a bee trying to get into your glass of lovely wine, you get upset and shout "BEE NO!" What's the Spanish word for *wine*? That's right — **vino**!

In **por favor**, *please*, the word **favor** looks the same as English "favor". As you say it, think of the expression "Do me a favor!"

Mental gymnastics 1

Look at the words below, then close your eyes and imagine you're at a bar in Mexico. Using the easy "GREEN FOR GO AHEAD" words and the "YELLOW FOR WAIT AND THINK" words, say to yourself the Spanish words for:

a soda   a wine   a bottle   mineral water

a tea   a coffee   a Coke®   please

Red
FOR STOP, THINK, MAKE A LINK

2

Listen to these words on CD1 and practice saying them.

una cerveza (*oo*-na sair-**be**-sa) a beer

un jugo (oon **hoo**-go) a juice

de naranja (*de na-**ran**-kha*) of orange

Learning red words the easy way

To learn these words you're going to link them to a memorable image and make a mental picture. We'll suggest an image for each drink, but you should create one of your own that works for you. Remember, the more bizarre, funny, or even vulgar the image, the better you'll remember it!

The Spanish word for *beer* is **cerveza**. It's quite unlike the English word, but link the sound with an image. A gentleman ('SIR'), who sings BASS in his local choir is standing at a bar enjoying a beer — 'AH!' SIR-BASS-AH.

In Spanish, *orange juice* is **jugo de naranja**. Imagine a wrestler called HUGO with a bright orange hat, squeezing an enormous orange with his big hands and pouring all the juice into a jug.

Mental gymnastics 2

Look at the pictures below, write their Spanish names underneath and say them. If you've forgotten any of the words, go back and check, and then take a few seconds more to visualize the images suggested above. It doesn't matter if you don't get the spelling right: saying them is much more important.

1. una botella de .... mineral

2. un ....

3. una ....

4. un ....

5. un jugo de ....

6. un ....

7. una ....

8. un ....

Let's get a drink

You've just arrived in Mexico. Use your imagination to picture yourself there: it's a lovely sunny afternoon, you can feel the sun on your skin and smell the scent of the flowers, and you feel relaxed. You're walking along a beach and you see a bar. Yes, you fancy a drink: maybe a nice cold beer, a fresh orange juice or Coke® ... or maybe a cup of freshly ground coffee ... or just a bottle of refreshing mineral water.
You choose!

In the following exercises the handsome *waiter* — **mesero** — greets Ms. Velvet and asks her what she'd like. You'll hear how she asks him for her drink and then you'll ask for a drink yourself.

> **Buenos días, ¿qué deseaba?**

> ...

3

Look at the pictures of all the drinks Ms. Velvet could be asking for. Then listen to four conversations and identify the drinks she does ask for. Mark each drink as you hear it. You may want to listen to the conversations more than once.

a. ☐   b. ☐   c. ☐

d. ☐   e. ☐   f. ☐

g. ☐   h. ☐

4

Now listen to the names of the other four drinks and try to identify them. Note down the letters of the matching pictures above.

1. ☐   2. ☐   3. ☐   4. ☐

Check your answers to listening exercises 3 and 4 at www.collinslanguage.com/revolution How many answers did you get right? All of them? BRILLIANT! Most of them? WELL DONE! Don't worry if you made a few mistakes. Let's keep on practicing.

5

Now you'll hear the names of all the drinks in the pictures in order, starting with **un café** *a coffee*. Listen to them again and repeat each one after you hear it.

6

It's your turn to take the place of Ms. Velvet and ask for some drinks. On CD1 you'll hear four conversations: after the **mesero** asks you what you'd like, there's a pause to give you time to ask for the drink shown below. Then you'll hear the correct answer.

1.   2.   3.   4.

7

Can you remember the names of the drinks that WEREN'T in the conversations you've just practiced? You'll probably remember some of them, if not all. Look at the drawings and say the words aloud, then listen to them on CD1.

1.   2.   3.   4.

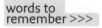

Botanas *(bo-**ta**-nas)*

Snacks

Now you know how to buy **bebidas** in a bar.
Let's turn our attention to **botanas**, *snacks*.

Green
FOR GO AHEAD

guacamole *(gooa-ka-**mo**-le)* guacamole

tortilla *(to-**tee**-ya)* tortilla (pancake made from cornmeal or wheat flour)

tacos *(**ta**-kos)* tacos (tortilla folded into a roll with a filling)

These words are the same or nearly the same in English and Spanish (although the pronunciation is slightly different).

Did you know?

Botanas

Botanas are small portions of food served with drinks in bars. Botanas are eaten before lunch or dinner to whet the appetite, and they are also a social institution. Over botanas, business deals are closed, friends exchange gossip and co-workers relax together.

Now let's look at some more words for snacks.

Yellow
FOR WAIT
AND THINK

tostada *(tos-**ta**-da)* flat tortilla, toasted or deep fried

flauta *(**flau**-ta)* crisp-fried, stuffed corn tortilla

Flautas are so called because they are long, thin, and cylindrical in shape so they look like flutes.

  8

Listen to the green and yellow words on CD1 and practice saying them.

Mental gymnastics 3

Close your eyes and imagine you're in a bar in Mexico. Using the easy "GREEN FOR GO AHEAD" words and the "YELLOW FOR WAIT AND THINK" words, say to yourself the Spanish words for:

flauta   tortilla   guacamole   tostada   tacos

camarones *(ka-ma-**ro**-nes)* shrimp

queso *(**ke**-so)* cheese

Red

FOR STOP, THINK, MAKE A LINK

 9

Listen to these words on CD1 and practice saying them.

Learning red words the easy way

Put your visualization hat back on to get these words lodged in your memory.

Camarones is unlike any English word, so use your imagination. Imagine a football team, the "California Camarones." The logo on their sweatshirts is a shrimp, and as they run onto the pitch the crowd roars "California Camarones!". Close your eyes: can you hear the crowd roaring "California Camarones!"?

In Spanish, *cheese* is **queso** — oKAY, SO you want cheese with that?

Mental gymnastics 4

The first letter of the botanas is given: fill in the missing letters. In Spanish, **ch** and **ll** are single letters.

1. c ....   5. g ....

2. t ....   6. f ....

3. q ....   7. t ....

4. t ....

10

Check your answers to Mental gymnastics 4 at **www.collinslanguage.com/revolution** and correct your spelling if necessary. Then listen to the words on CD1 and practice saying them.

Tony's Tip

Repeat and succeed

If you revise something five times over six months, it will stick in your brain **for ever**!

Five times repetition = long-term memory

1st repetition: **an hour or so** after learning something
2nd repetition: **a day** later
3rd repetition: **a week** later
4th repetition: **a month** later
5th repetition: **six months** later

Time for a snack

La señora Velvet has been drinking a great vino, enjoying the view and letting her mind wander. She's starting to feel hungry, and into her mind comes the image of a lovely botanas tree, its branches hung with delicious botanas of tortilla, shrimps, flautas, cheese, tacos, tostadas and guacamole.

11

Listen to the botanas tree saying the names of the botanas hanging from its branches. In the boxes beside the pictures on page 29, write a number 1 to 7 to show the order in which you hear them on CD1. You may want to listen more than once. Remember to check your answers at **www.collinslanguage.com/revolution**.

Luckily, the handsome mesero is approaching. He asks her if she'd like a botana ...

12

Listen to four conversations on CD1 and identify the botana la señora Velvet is asking for in each one. Write their names in English.

1.
2.
3.
4.

 13

Now it's your turn to ask for a botana. You'll hear four conversations: after the mesero asks you what you'd like, there's a pause for you to ask for the botana below. Then you'll hear the correct answer.

1. shrimp

2. guacamole

3. cheese

4. tostada

14

Listen to the botanas tree saying the names of its "fruits" and write them in Spanish in the order in which you hear them.

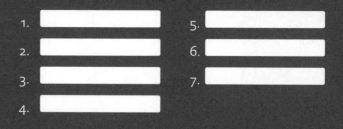

1.
2.
3.
4.

5.
6.
7.

 15

Listen to four more conversations and write in Spanish the bebida and botana each person asks for. You may want to listen more than once.

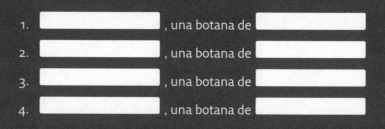

1.   , una botana de
2.   , una botana de
3.   , una botana de
4.   , una botana de

The check, please!

It's getting late: time for Ms. Velvet to ask for the check before leaving.

la cuenta *(la **kwen**-ta)* the check

La cuenta is literally "the account." To ask for the check, simply say **La cuenta, por favor**. And here are two important words you'll need:

gracias *(**gra**-syas)* thank you

adiós *(a-**dyos**)* goodbye

At this stage, don't worry about not knowing any numbers in Spanish, because the check will show the amount to pay. But do remember to say **Gracias y adiós**.

 16

Listen to the waiter and Ms. Velvet using these phrases and practice saying them.

You've been learning how to ask for bebidas and botanas in a bar. Now you're going to use a Mind Map to help you remember the words you've just learned.

Mind Map it!

Look at our first Mind Map. Then take a sheet of paper and some colored pens and draw your own. If you know the names of other botanas or bebidas, add them to your Mind Map.

GUACAMOLE

TORTILLA

TACOS

TOSTADA

FLAUTA

BOTANAS

BEBIDAS

En el bar

COCA-COLA

REFRESCO

TÉ

AGUA MINERAL

VINO

Tony's Tip

Mind Mapping

The Mind Map is the king of memory tools! It helps you think, learn, imagine, remember, and sort information.

Mind Map + Associations + Imagination = Success

use CD2
for more audio practice and revision

2

En taxi al hotel

By the end of this unit you will be able to:

- Take a taxi
- Check into a hotel
- Use the numbers 0-10
- Say "good afternoon" and "good evening"
- Guess the meaning of dozens of new
  Spanish words

words to
remember >>>

¡Taxi! *(tak-see)*

Taxi!

In this unit you'll learn how to take a taxi from the airport to your hotel and book in. Your first step is to memorize some words and expressions you'll need at the airport.

Green
FOR GO AHEAD

 17

Listen to these
words on CD1
and practice
saying them.

el taxi *(el **tak**-see)* taxi

el tren *(el tren)* train

el autobús *(el aw-to-**boos**)* bus

el hotel *(el o-**tel**)* hotel

el centro *(el **sen**-tro)* center

el aeropuerto *(el a-e-ro-**pwair**-to)* airport

la estación de tren
*(la es-ta-**syon** de tren)* train station

la estación de autobuses
*(la es-ta-**syon** de ow-to-**boo**-ses)* bus station

pesos *(**pe**-sos)* pesos (Mexican currency)

cero *(**se**-ro)* zero

Remember, words in green are the same or nearly the same in English and Spanish. Although these words look much the same as English words, in most cases they aren't pronounced the same way.

Nuts & bolts
masculine and feminine

There are two words for *the* in Spanish, as you've seen with the green words above: **el taxi**, **el hotel**, but **la estación**.

That's because in Spanish all nouns (words for people, places, and things) are either masculine (**el**) or feminine (**la**). It's easy to guess that *woman* is feminine — **la mujer** — but there's often no logical reason why a word should be masculine or feminine.

A useful clue is that almost all Spanish nouns ending in **-o** are masculine and most of those ending in **-a** are feminine.

Tony's Tip

Masculine or Feminine?

Here's an easy and fun way to remember whether to put **el** or **la** in front of a Spanish word. Pick a super-masculine figure and associate him with every masculine word. Do the same with the feminine words and a super-feminine figure.

Suppose you've chosen El Zorro as your masculine figure and somebody called Doña María, dressed in a Mexican traditional dress selling fruit, as your feminine one.

For **el hotel**, imagine El Zorro riding his horse into the lobby of a luxury hotel and picking up the room key with his sword.

For **la estación de tren**, picture Doña María selling fruit on the platform as your train pulls in.

Mental gymnastics 1

Give yourself 20 seconds to memorize the "GREEN FOR GO AHEAD" words. Then cover them up and write down as many as you can. Include **el** or **la** where needed and link your super-masculine and super-feminine figures with the words. You could organize them under these headings:

Means of transportation   *Places*   *Money and numbers*

check your answers at
www.collinslanguage.com/revolution

A working relationship (1)

There are lots of Spanish words that end in **-ción**, like **estación**. Can you guess what **recepción** and **atracción** mean? That's right: the English equivalents end in *-tion*. You've added dozens of words to your Spanish vocabulary at a stroke!

Now let's look at the numbers 1 to 10.

Red
FOR STOP, THINK, MAKE A LINK

  18

Listen to the numbers and practice saying them.

1	**uno** *(oo-no)*	6	**seis** *(seys)*
2	**dos** *(dos)*	7	**siete** *(sye-te)*
3	**tres** *(tres)*	8	**ocho** *(o-cho)*
4	**cuatro** *(kwa-tro)*	9	**nueve** *(nwe-be)*
5	**cinco** *(seen-ko)*	10	**diez** *(dyes)*

Learning red words the easy way

Here's a set of visualizations you could use to remember the numbers. There's plenty happening down on the farm …

1	**uno**	"OOH, NO!" says the farmer, with one foot on the stile.
2	**dos**	"Two twins are DOSSing in the barn."
3	**tres**	A trio of trekkers are TRESpassing on the farm.
4	**cuatro**	A quartet of ducks quack along to a Suzi QUATRO number.
5	**cinco**	I have SEEN COats on five forlorn shorn sheep.
6	**seis**	Six hissing swans SAY "SSS".
7	**siete**	Seven satisfied rabbits, SEE, ATE A carrot

each.

8	**ocho**	Eight crows wATCH Overhead, circling in figures of eight.
9	**nueve**	Nine day-old ducklings make NEW WAVEs on the pond.
10	**diez**	Ten tractors lose the ploughing match to a Citroën DS.

These numbers, plus **cero**, are all you need. In an emergency, if you can't work out how to say "three hundred and eighteen," just say the figures separately: *three one eight*, **tres uno ocho.**

Mental gymnastics 2

Read the list of numbers and their associated images again, taking a few seconds to picture each one. Cover up the numbers or close your eyes and, as you recall each image, say the number aloud.

Mental gymnastics 3

Read these sequences of numbers aloud in Spanish. Keep practicing until you can say them quickly and fluently. You could listen to CD1 track 18 again first, to remind yourself of the pronunciation. Then, if you like, write the numbers out and check your spelling.

0	10	5 - 4 - 3 - 2 - 1
1 - 2 - 3	1 - 3 - 5 - 7 - 9	0
4 - 5 - 6	2 - 4 - 6 - 8 - 10	
7 - 8 - 9	10 - 9 - 8 - 7 - 6	

Let's take a taxi

To hail a taxi in the street, just shout **¡Taxi!** You can also phone for one, but most of the time you'll find taxis waiting for you outside el aeropuerto, la estación, or el hotel.

Mr. and Mrs. Herbert, a couple from the United States, **los Estados Unidos**, have just arrived in la Ciudad de México. This is their first holiday in Mexico and they're really looking forward to practising their Spanish, as well as seeing the sights. After collecting their luggage in the airport, they want to find a taxi to take them to their hotel. No problem: they follow the signs saying **salida** *exit* and there, right in front of them, is **la parada de taxis** *the taxi stand*. La señora Herbert goes up to the first taxi, beckoning to her husband to follow. Let's see how **el señor y la señora** Herbert get on.

Mental gymnastics 4

Look at the cartoons and then write down the Spanish phrases la señora
Herbert and the taxi driver — el taxista — use to say the following:

Good afternoon. ....

Are you free? ....

Yes. ....

Where do you want to go? ....

To the Hotel Sol. ....

Please ....

Thank you ....

How much is it? ....

19 **Listen to the conversation while you look at the
cartoons. If you like, you could read la señora
Herbert's lines aloud as you hear them. You may
want to listen more than once.**

Nuts & bolts
questions and exclamations

In Spanish, question and exclamation marks appear at the
beginning as well as the end of a question or exclamation.
At the beginning they are written upside down (¿ ¡) and at
the end the right way up (? !).

◎ **20**

It's your turn to take the place of la señora Herbert in the conversation. On CD1 her lines have been replaced by pauses, to give you time to speak. First you'll hear the taxi driver say **Buenas tardes, señora**, followed by a pause for you to respond. Then you'll hear the correct answer. If you need help, look at the cartoons again. You may want to do this exercise more than once.

◎ **21**

This time la señora Herbert and her husband — **su esposo** — get into the taxi together. Listen to their conversation.

Did you know?

Taxis

There are several kinds of taxis in Mexico City, the most common of which are two or four-door models painted green. The most representative of these is the VW bug, called a *vocho* in Mexico City slang.

It's important before getting into a taxi that you verify the vehicle's license plates start with an L or an S; otherwise, don't get in.

There are tourist taxis (*taxis turísticos*) at the airport and certain hotels.

Mental gymnastics 5

The new conversation is almost identical to the first one, but not quite. In the first conversation, the taxi driver asked **¿Adónde va usted?** This time he says something slightly different. Read the conversation below, compare it with the first one in the cartoons, and underline the words that have changed. Why do you think they are different? Read the "NUTS & BOLTS" to check.

Taxista:	**Buenas tardes.**
Señora Herbert:	**Buenas tardes. ¿Está libre?**
Taxista:	**Sí. ¿Adónde van ustedes?**
Señora Herbert:	**Al Hotel Sol, por favor.**
Taxista:	**Este es el Hotel Sol.**
Señora Herbert:	**Gracias. ¿Cuánto es?**
Taxista:	**Son doscientos pesos.**
Señor y señora Herbert:	**Adiós. Buenas tardes**.

Nuts & bolts
usted and ustedes

In the first conversation, the taxi driver had only one passenger and he asked **¿Adónde va usted?** In the second conversation, the driver has two passengers and he asks both of them **¿Adónde van ustedes?**

The word **usted** *you (singular)* is used to talk to one person politely and **ustedes** *you (plural)* to talk to two or more people politely. **Va** and **van** are the words for *go* that are used with **usted** and **ustedes**.

To the station!

You may want to take a taxi or a bus to somewhere other than your hotel. When asked **¿Adónde va usted?** la señora Herbert said **Al Hotel Sol,** but if she wanted to go to the train station she would say **A la estación de tren**.

Mental gymnastics 6

Do you remember the names of the five places you learned at the beginning of this unit? Write down as many as you can and then check them in the "GREEN FOR GO AHEAD" section.

Mental gymnastics 7

Write the answers to the questions in Spanish.

1. **¿Adónde va usted?** *to the airport* ....

2. **¿Adónde va usted?** *to the bus station* ....

3. **¿Adónde va usted?** *to the Hotel Mar* ....

Nuts & bolts
al ... and a la ...

Al and **a la** both mean *to the:* **al** is **a** *to* combined with **el**.
So *to the hotel* is **al hotel** and *to the train station* is **a la estación de tren**

Mental gymnastics 8

Complete these two conversations in Spanish.

1.
Señora Herbert:	....
Taxista:	**Sí. ¿Adónde van ustedes?**
Señora Herbert:	.... **Hotel Sol.**
Taxista:	**Este es el Hotel Sol.**
Señora Herbert:	**Gracias.** ....
Taxista:	**Son doscientos** ....
Señora y Señor Herbert:	**Adiós. Buenas tardes.**

2.
Señor Herbert:	**¿Está libre?**
Taxista:	**Sí. ¿Adónde van ustedes?**
Señor Herbert:	.... **la estación de tren.**
Taxista:	**Esta es la estación.**
Señor Herbert:	....
Taxista:	.... **doscientos pesos.**
Señor Herbert:	**Adiós. Buenas tardes.**

🔘 **22**

Now listen to the two conversations and say the passengers' lines aloud. There are pauses to give you time to speak, and then you'll hear the correct answer. You can check your answers in the transcript at www.collinslanguage.com/revolution

go to
www.collinslanguage.com/revolution
for extra activities

cuarenta y siete 47

words to remember >>>

En el hotel *(en el o-**tel**)*

At the hotel

Before finding out how el señor y la señora Herbert are doing, let's look at some words you'll find useful when booking into a hotel.

Green
FOR GO AHEAD

doble *(**do**-ble)* double

el pasaporte *(el pa-sa-**por**-te)* passport

Yellow
FOR WAIT
AND THINK

la habitación *(la a-bee-ta-**syon**)* room

individual *(een-dee-bee-**dwal**)* single

How to remember yellow words

To learn these words, find something that connects the English with the Spanish. The word for *room*, **habitación**, may remind you of "habitation" or "habitat," a place to live. In a hotel context, **individual** means *single (room)*, but it also has the same meaning as the English *individual*.

Red
FOR STOP, THINK,
MAKE A LINK

 23

**Listen to all
these words
and practice
saying them.**

el baño *(el **ba**-nyo)* bath

la cama *(la **ka**-ma)* bed

la noche *(la **no**-che)* night

Learning red words the easy way
To learn these red words, link them to a memorable image.
For **la cama** you could imagine Doña María, lying on a bed
reading the KAMA Sutra. And for **el baño** try picturing
El Zorro playing the BANJO in a bath.

Mental gymnastics 9

Give yourself 60 seconds to solve these anagrams of the hotel
words you've just learned.

1. CHENO .... 4. OBAÑ ....

2. ALVINUDIDI .... 5. CIBAHAITÓN ....

3. MACA .... 6. LOBED ....

Tony's Tip

Rest and learn best

Take frequent study breaks to keep your mind fresh,
even if you don't feel tired. We tend to remember best the
things we studied first and last in a session, and regular
breaks give you more "firsts" and "lasts"!

So you could take a break now before moving on.

Booking in

El señor y la señora Herbert have arrived at the Hotel Sol, where they have *a room with bath* **una habitación con baño** booked *for three nights* **por tres noches**.
El señor Herbert goes up to the desk to check in and the charming receptionist says good evening.

Mental gymnastics 10

Complete the conversation.

Recepcionista: **Buenas noches.**

Señor Herbert: **Buenas** ....

Recepcionista: **¿Qué deseaba?**

Señor Herbert: **Una** .... **doble con dos camas, por favor.**

Recepcionista: **¿Tiene reservación?**

Señor Herbert: **Sí. Los señores Herbert.**

Recepcionista: **Herbert ... ¿Por cuántas noches?**

Señor Herbert: **Por** .... (3) ....

Recepcionista: **¿Con baño?**

Señor Herbert: **Sí,** ....

Recepcionista: **Muy bien. Su pasaporte, por favor.**

24

Listen to the conversation you've just completed. If you like, you could read el señor Herbert's lines aloud as you hear them. You may want to listen more than once.

25

Now it's your turn. You've booked a single room with bath, for one night. Listen to the receptionist and respond in the pauses. Then you'll hear the correct answer.

Nuts & bolts
¿Por cuántas noches?
For how many nights?

una noche = *one night*
tres noches = *three nights*

una cama = *one bed*
dos camas = *two beds*

Mind Map it!

Draw your own Mind Map for el hotel. Add the hotel words
you've learned in this unit and any others you know.
Remember to use color and images as visual aids.

INDIVIDUAL

HABITACIÓN   DOBLE

¿NOCHES?

EL HOTEL

Use flash cards to memorize

Tony's Tip

Get some blank index cards. Write a new Spanish word on
one side of each card and its English translation on the
other. Always include **el** or **la** and imagine what El Zorro
and Doña María are doing. You can draw your memorable
image on the card if you like. Test yourself by looking at the
English words and trying to translate them.

Remember to shuffle the cards regularly!

use CD2
for more audio practice and revision

3

A la oficina de turismo

By the end of this unit you will be able to:

- Order breakfast
- Ask for and understand directions
- Find out about accommodation
- Book a place to stay

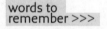

words to remember >>>

El desayuno *(el de-sa-**yoo**-no)*
Breakfast

Green
FOR GO AHEAD

el chocolate *(el cho-ko-**la**-te)* (drinking) chocolate

los cereales *(los se-re-**a**-les)* cereal

el yogur *(el yo-**goor**)* yogurt

el limón *(el lee-**mon**)* lemon

la fruta *(la **froo**-ta)* fruit

la tortilla *(la tor-**tee**-ya)* tortilla (See Unit 1)

la mermelada *(la mair-me-**la**-da)* jam

Yellow
FOR WAIT
AND THINK

To remember this word, think of the English word *marmalade.*

(◎) **26**

Listen to these words and practice saying them.

Nuts & bolts
singular and plural

Singular = one thing:

el limón **la tortilla**

Plural = more than one thing:

los limones **las tortillas**

In the plural, **el** and **la** change to **los** and **las**.
Words ending in a vowel **(a, e, i, o, u)** add -**s**.
Words ending in a consonant **(n, r, s ...)** add -**es**.

Red
FOR STOP, THINK,
MAKE A LINK

 27

Listen to these words and practice saying them.

la leche *(la le-che)* milk

la mantequilla *(la man-te-kee-ya)* butter

el desayuno *(el de-sa-yoo-no)* breakfast

el pan *(el pan)* bread

los cuernitos *(los kuer-ni-tos)* croissants

To memorize these red words, associate them with a memorable image. For the word **desayuno** imagine yourself asking your friend "DES, ARE YOU NO having breakfast?" To remember **pan**, imagine yourself frying a loaf of bread in a PAN.

Cuernitos means little horns in Spanish because in fact croissants look like a pair of horns. So next time try to remember that before you have your beef burger for lunch you need to have **cuernitos** first for breakfast.

Make up your own images for the rest of these words and you'll always remember them! Link them with your masculine and feminine characters, too.

Nuts & bolts
con, y

Use the word **con** *(kon)* to say *with*, as in **café con leche** *coffee with milk*.

Use **y** *(ee)* and to link two or more things, as in **pan con mantequilla y mermelada** *bread with butter and jam*.

Mental gymnastics 1

Give yourself 30 seconds to memorize the lists of words you've just seen. Then look at the pictures below and write their names. Include **el** or **la**, **los** or **las** — think of your super-masculine and super-feminine figures.

1. ....

2. ....

3. ....

4. ....

5. ....

Tony's Tip

Get up and move about!

Who said you had to be sitting at your desk to learn a language? Next time you have breakfast, try writing a breakfast menu with all the items you've just learned.

Prepare a Mexican breakfast, where coffee, fruit and cereal become **café, fruta, y cereales**. You could even have a go at making **quesadillas** (cornbread filled with cheese) — they're a perfect snack for anytime!

Mental gymnastics 2

Give yourself 60 seconds to read again all the green and red words you have learned. Think about what you'd like for breakfast and combine the various things on offer in any order you like, using **con** and **y**.

1. cereales .... *con leche* ....

2. pan ....

3. café ....

4. yogur ....

Mind Map it!

Extend the Mind Map with as many words as you can remember from this unit. Can you work out what **beber** and **comer** mean?

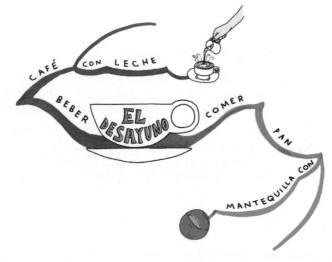

Time for breakfast

After a good night's sleep, el señor y la señora Herbert
have come down to the breakfast lounge of the hotel for
el desayuno.

Mental gymnastics 3

In Unidad 1, En el bar, you learned the names of some bebidas. See if you can
remember them by recalling the associations you made. Write the words
beside the drawings below. If you've forgotten some of them, just go back to
Unidad 1 and find them. You could add them to your breakfast Mind Map.

1. ....

2. ....

3. ....

4. ....

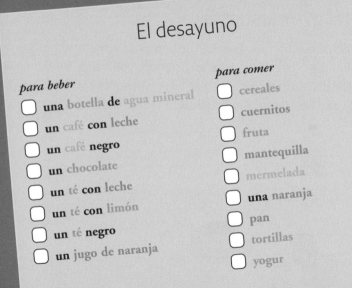

28 El señor y la señora Herbert are reading the breakfast menu. Listen to their conversation with el mesero and mark the items they choose for breakfast. Use a ✔ for la señora Herbert and a ✗ for el señor Herbert.

El desayuno

para beber

- [ ] una botella de agua mineral
- [ ] un café con leche
- [ ] un café negro
- [ ] un chocolate
- [ ] un té con leche
- [ ] un té con limón
- [ ] un té negro
- [ ] un jugo de naranja

para comer

- [ ] cereales
- [ ] cuernitos
- [ ] fruta
- [ ] mantequilla
- [ ] mermelada
- [ ] una naranja
- [ ] pan
- [ ] tortillas
- [ ] yogur

Nuts & bolts
un and una *(a, an)*

You met these words in Unidad 1. **Un**, like **el**, goes with masculine words, so **un** always goes with words associated with your strong masculine character. **Una**, like **la**, goes with feminine words, which are associated with your strong feminine character.

29

Now it's your turn to order el desayuno. Read the conversations below and write the answers in Spanish. Then listen to the conversations and act them out. There's a pause for you to answer and then you'll hear the correct answer.

1. Mesero: **Buenos días, ¿qué va a tomar?**
   Usted:
   Black coffee and a bottle of mineral water.
   Mesero: **¿Algo de comer? Tortillas, pan, cuernitos, cereales, yogur, fruta ...**
   Usted: **Hmm**
   Croissants, please.
   Mesero: **¿Mantequilla y mermelada?**
   Usted:
   Jam, please.

2. Mesero: **Buenos días, ¿qué va a tomar?**
   Usted:
   Coffee with milk and an orange juice.
   Mesero: **¿Algo de comer? Tortillas, pan, cuernitos, cereales, yogur, fruta ...**
   Usted: **Hmm**
   Fruit, yogurt and croissants.
   Mesero: **¿Mantequilla y mermelada?**
   Usted:
   Butter, please.

go to
www.collinslanguage.com/revolution
for extra activities

sesenta y uno 61

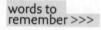 words to remember >>>

En la recepción *(en la re-sep-**syon**)*

In reception

Green
FOR GO AHEAD

la oficina de turismo
*(la o-fee-**see**-na de too-**rees**-mo)*
the tourist information office

un metro *(oon **me**-tro)* a meter

un minuto *(oon mee-**noo**-to)* a minute

Yellow
FOR WAIT
AND THINK

primero, primera *(pree-**me**-ro, pree-**me**-ra)* first

segundo, segunda
*(se-**goon**-do, se-**goon**-da)* second

tercero, tercera *(tair-**se**-ro, tair-**se**-ra)* third

Primero, *first*, is related to the English words "premier" and "prime" (as in "Prime Minister").
Segundo looks and sounds a lot like "second," and you can associate **tercero** with the related English word "tertiary."

Red

FOR STOP, THINK,
MAKE A LINK

 30

Listen to the
green, yellow
and red words
and practice
saying them.

la calle *(la **ka**-ye)* street

cerca de *(**sair**-ka de)* near (to)

aquí *(a-**kee**)* here

todo derecho *(**to**-do de-**re**-cho)* straight ahead

a la derecha *(a la de-**re**-cha)* on/to the right

a la izquierda *(a la ees-**kyair**-da)* on/to the left

Making a scene!

Here's a visualization to help you remember these words.
You have a friend called Callie who likes to relax with a
drink after work.

Imagine Callie in a long straight street, **calle**, where the
DIRECT route is **todo derecho** ("Todo derecho is directo!").
There's a bar on the right-hand side and a shop on the
left. The bar is run by DEREK and is called **La Derecha**;
the shop belongs to LIZ KEY and is called, predictably,
La Izquierda. For Callie, going to the bar is always the
RIGHT choice, and if she has any money LEFT she goes
to the shop!

Is there ...?

Pablo and Cristina, a young Mexican couple, are spending a few days in the city before joining some friends in Mérida. They ask the hotel receptionist if there's **una oficina de turismo** nearby where they can book the next stage of their holiday.

Mental gymnastics 4

Match the maps with the conversations below.

  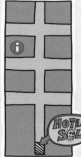 

a   b   c   d

1. ....

Pablo:	**Por favor, ¿hay una oficina de turismo cerca de aquí?**
Recepcionista:	**Sí, hay una a dos minutos de aquí.**
Pablo:	**¿Dónde?**
Recepcionista:	**Saliendo del hotel, la primera calle a la izquierda.**

2. ....

Pablo: **Por favor, ¿hay una oficina de turismo cerca de aquí?**

Recepcionista: **Sí, hay una a diez minutos de aquí.**

Pablo: **¿Dónde?**

Recepcionista: **Saliendo del hotel, la tercera calle a la derecha.**

3. ....

Pablo: **Por favor, ¿hay una oficina de turismo cerca de aquí?**

Recepcionista: **Sí, hay una a cinco minutos de aquí.**

Pablo: **¿Dónde?**

Recepcionista: **Saliendo del hotel, la segunda calle a la izquierda.**

4. ....

Pablo: **Por favor, ¿hay una oficina de turismo cerca de aquí?**

Recepcionista: **Sí, hay una a diez metros de aquí.**

Pablo: **¿Dónde?**

Recepcionista: **Saliendo del hotel, todo derecho.**

Nuts & bolts
¿Hay ...?

¿Hay (aee)**?** Is there/Are there? is one of those words that you'll find yourself using over and over again, to find a place or an object. Simply replace **una oficina de turismo** with whatever it is you want to find.

¿Hay
$\begin{cases} \text{un bar} \\ \text{una estación de tren} \\ \text{un hotel} \end{cases}$
cerca de aquí?

31 Listen to two more conversations and mark on the maps where the oficina de turismo is.

32 Listen to four conversations and complete the table in English.

	Place	Distance	Directions
1.	bus station	7 mins	2nd street on left
2.			
3.			
4.			

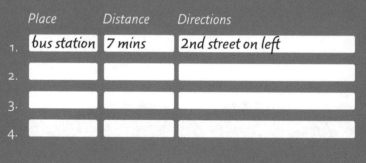

Tony's Tip

Repeat and succeed

five times repetition = long-term memory

Every time you practice and review your new language, you'll be making deeper, wider, and more permanent pathways of language learning between your brain cells.

words to remember >>>

Una reservación

*(oo-na re-**sair**-ba-si-on)* A reservation

Green
FOR GO AHEAD

el precio *(el **pre**-syo)* price

el día *(el **dee**-a)* day

Yellow
FOR WAIT
AND THINK

el nombre *(el **nom**-bre)* (first) name

el apellido *(el a-pe-**yee**-do)* surname

la casa *(la **ka**-sa)* house

la llegada *(la ye-**ga**-da)* arrival

Red
FOR STOP, THINK,
MAKE A LINK

la salida *(la sa-**lee**-da)* departure, exit

 33

Listen to all the words you've just seen and practice saying them.

Create your own images and associations to help you memorize these words, and remember Doña María and El Zorro!

Somewhere to stay

Pablo and Cristina are in the tourist information office. They want to book **una casa de campo**, *a rural cottage*, in Mérida. They ask the employee to find out if there's una casa de campo available in their chosen area.

 34

Revise the numbers you learned in Unidad 2 and then listen to the conversation and answer the questions below.

1. Which area do Cristina and Pablo want to visit?

2. How many days do they want to stay?

3. Which dates in July?

Making sense of what you hear

The first thing the person behind the oficina de turismo desk is going to say is **¿En qué puedo ayudarles?** — literally *In what can I help you?*

You've probably never seen or heard this sentence before, so you don't know exactly what it means, but that doesn't matter: you can guess the meaning of what you hear because of the situation in which it is said. This is a really useful trick when learning a foreign language!

The employee has given them a leaflet about una casa de campo. The photo is impressive and there's a brief description. Have a look at it and see how much you can understand.

CASA DE CAMPO "SAN JOSÉ"

Número de personas: **4**

Número de recámaras: **2**

Superficie: **750 m²**

Precio Máx.:
$ 800 por día (temporada alta)

Precio Min.:
$ 600 por día (temporada baja)

Preciosa casa de campo restaurada y completamente equipada. Situación privilegiada a las afueras de Mérida.

There's almost nothing to translate, is there? You can work out what **superficie** means from the answer, 750m². **Temporada alta/baja** is *high/low season*. **Restaurada** means *restored*: when you go to a restaurant, your strength is being restored!

Cristina and Pablo like the look of the house and ask the employee to make an online booking for them.

⊙ 35

Look at the booking form. What do you think Forma de pago means? Listen to the conversation and fill in the form.

Nombre:	Apellido:	Llegada:		Salida:	
Cristina	García		julio		julio

Personas:	Número de teléfono:	Número de celular:

Forma de pago:

Did you know?

Accommodation in Mexico

There's no shortage of accommodation in México, ranging from the basic to the luxurious — but if you want to give yourself a treat, book into an **hacienda**. **Haciendas** are privately owned quality hotels in converted historic buildings, so every **hacienda** is unique. They generally offer fine cuisine inspired by traditional local fare.

Mental gymnastics 5

You probably worked out from the answer, Visa, that **forma de pago** means *method of payment*. Now read and practice the conversation.

Oficina de turismo: **¿Sí?**
Cristina: **¿Podría reservar la casa?**

Oficina de turismo: **Sí. ¿Su nombre, por favor?**
Cristina: **Cristina.**

Oficina de turismo: **¿Apellido?**
Cristina: **García.**

Oficina de turismo: **¿Llegada?**
Cristina: **El cinco de julio.**

Oficina de turismo: **¿Salida?**
Cristina: **El ocho.**

Oficina de turismo: **¿Número de personas?**
Cristina: **Cuatro.**

Oficina de turismo: **¿Teléfono?**
Cristina: **98765432**

Oficina de turismo: **¿Celular?**
Cristina: **8112935642**

Oficina de turismo: **¿Forma de pago?**
Cristina: **Visa.**

Oficina de turismo: **Muy bien. Reservada. ¿Algo más?**

36   Use the details on the form to complete the
     conversation. Then listen and act it out. There are
     pauses for you to give your answers.

Nombre:	Apellido:	Llegada:	Salida:
Chris	Bell	3 · julio ·	9 · julio ·

Personas:	Número de teléfono:	Número de celular:
2 ·	91140392	075348217

Forma de pago: Visa ·

Oficina de turismo: **¿Sí?**
Usted:
Oficina de turismo: **Sí. ¿Su nombre, por favor?**
Usted:
Oficina de turismo: **¿Apellido?**
Usted:
Oficina de turismo: **¿Llegada?**
Usted:
Oficina de turismo: **¿Salida?**
Usted:
Oficina de turismo: **¿Número de personas?**
Usted
Oficina de turismo: **¿Teléfono?**
Usted:
Oficina de turismo: **¿Celular?**
Usted:
Oficina de turismo: **¿Forma de pago?**
Usted:
Oficina de turismo: **Muy bien. Reservada. ¿Algo más?**

use CD2
for more audio practice and revision

4

Un fin de semana en la Ciudad de México

By the end of this unit you will be able to:

- Find out about places to visit
- Say you don't understand
- Use the numbers 11-30 and the days of the week
- Understand opening and closing times
- Buy tickets

words to remember >>>

Información *(een-for-ma-**syon**)*

Information

Green
FOR GO AHEAD

 37

Listen to these words and practice saying them.

los museos *(los-moo-**se**-os)* museums

los monumentos
*(los mo-noo-**men**-tos)* (historic) monuments

los parques *(los **par**-kes)* parks

los cafés *(los ka-**fes**)* cafés

los bares *(los **ba**-res)* bars

los teatros *(los te-**a**-tros)* theaters

los conciertos *(los kon-**syair**-tos)* concerts

These words for places to visit are all masculine, so associate them with El Zorro or your own super-masculine character.

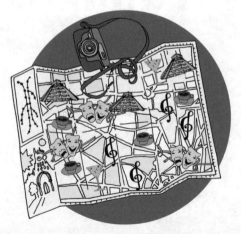

Mental gymnastics 1

Rewrite the "GREEN FOR GO AHEAD" words as if there were only one of each thing.

el museo

....

....

Mental gymnastics 2

Answer each question with one of the words you've just learnt,
as in the example.

1. Where would you go for a walk?   *un parque*

2. Where could you go to hear live music?   ....

3. If you want a cup of coffee, where can you get one?   ....

4. Where can you enjoy a refreshing beer?   ....

5. Where would you go to watch a play?   ....

6. Where would you expect to see works of art exhibited?   ....

What is there to see?

John and Michael, two colleagues from Seattle, are in la Ciudad de México on business and have **el fin de semana** *the weekend* free. They're studying Spanish with the *Collins Language Revolution*, and this is a great opportunity to practice their Spanish while exploring the city. They haven't had much time to prepare, so they head for una oficina de turismo.

Before going in, John wants to practice the phrases he may need, so he extracts a few flash cards from his backpack and asks a surprised Michael to test him.

a

Queríamos información sobre la Ciudad de México

(ke-**ree**-a-mos een-for-ma-**syon** **so**-bre la siu-dad de **me**-ksi-ko)

b

Qué ver y qué hacer

(ke bair ee ke a-**sair**)

Mental gymnastics 3

See if you can match the Spanish phrases on John's cards with the English ones below. Check your answers and then practice reading the phrases aloud.

Asking for information

1. How much does ... cost?
2. We'd like information about la Ciudad de México
3. What to see and do

To clarify

4. I don't speak much Spanish (literally: I speak little Spanish)
5. I don't understand
6. More slowly, please
7. What does ... mean?

c

¿Cuánto cuesta ...?

(**kwan**-to **kwes**-ta)

e

¿Qué significa ...?

(ke seeg-nee-**fee**-ka)

g

Más despacio, por favor

(mas des-**pa**-syo por fa-**bor**)

d

No entiendo

(no en-**tyen**-do)

f

Hablo poco español

(**a**-blo **po**-ko es-pa-**nyol**)

Feeling more confident, John leads the way into la oficina de turismo and goes up to the information desk.

38

Listen to John's conversation with the employee and answer the questions in English.

1. Which places does the employee mention when asked what to see and do in la Ciudad de México?

2. What is John interested in seeing?

3. What does the word **zona** mean?

How did you get on? There were quite a few unfamiliar words in that conversation. Check your answers at www.collinslanguage.com/revolution and then listen again to see how much more you can pick up.

John and Michael sit down to read the information about **Coyoacán** and **el Museo Frida Kahlo**.

Mental gymnastics 4

Read the leaflet opposite and see how much you can understand. Underline the words or expressions you're unsure of.

go to
www.collinslanguage.com/revolution
for extra activities

Mental gymnastics 5

Find the Spanish equivalents of the following in the leaflet. Check your answers and then read the leaflet again. Now that you know what the key words mean, how much more can you understand?

1. route
2. painting
3. sculpture
4. nature
5. areas
6. famous
7. itineraries
8. most

Coyoacán y el Museo Frida Kahlo

Coyoacán es una ruta única en la Ciudad de México.

Aquí, pintura y escultura, arquitectura y naturaleza se reúnen en una de las zonas más famosas de la Ciudad de México. Coyoacán es uno de los itinerarios con más carácter en esta ciudad capital.

Tomemos por ejemplo el Museo Frida Kahlo, también conocida como la Casa Azul.

Aquí están varias pinturas famosas de la artista.

words to
remember >>>

Días y horas *(dee-as ee o-ras)*

Days and hours

Yellow
FOR WAIT
AND THINK

 39

**Listen to
these words
and practice
saying them.**

el horario *(el o-ra-ryo)* opening hours

la entrada *(la en-tra-da)* ticket

gratis *(gra-tees)* free (of charge)

One word, many meanings

Horario is clearly related to **hora** *hour*. Here we're using it to mean *opening hours*, but it can also mean "timetable".

Similarly, **entrada** can mean not only *ticket*, but also "entrance", "hallway", "entry", "input" etc., depending on the context. In Spanish, as in English, many words have different meanings in different situations.

To remember **gratis**, think of the expression "Free, gratis, and for nothing!"

Red
FOR STOP, THINK,
MAKE A LINK

 40

Listen to
the days of
the week
and practice
saying them.

el lunes *(el **loo**-nes)* Monday

el martes *(el **mar**-tes)* Tuesday

el miércoles *(el **myair**-ko-les)* Wednesday

el jueves *(el **khwe**-bes)* Thursday

el viernes *(el **byair**-nes)* Friday

el sábado *(el **sa**-ba-do)* Saturday

el domingo *(el do-**meen**-go)* Sunday

el fin de semana *(el feen de se-**ma**-na)* the weekend

Los días de la semana

Here's a story to help you remember **los días de la semana**, *the days of the week*, but remember that the most effective associations are the ones you make yourself!

On Monday a bunch of LOONIES (**lunes**) prepared for a party at MARTY'S (**martes**) on Tuesday. The next day, Wednesday, they bumped into a shady character they had met at the party, called MURKY LES (**miércoles**). On Thursday this shady character took them to HUGH WEBB'S (**jueves**) cobwebby holiday cottage near Loch Ness, full of giant spiders. They stayed there until Friday, drinking BEER NESS (**viernes**). On Saturday everyone had a hangover and it waS A BAD DO (**sábado**), but they felt better when Plácido DOMINGO (**domingo**) turned up on Sunday and sang to them.

Mental gymnastics 6

Give yourself 30 seconds to complete the information.
If **lunes** is the first day of the week, then ...

1. *lunes*

6. ....

4. ....

3. ....

7. ....

5. ....

2. ....

Nuts & bolts
days of the week

The words **lunes**, **martes**, **miércoles**, **jueves**, and **viernes**
stay the same whether you are referring to ONE or SEVERAL **lunes**,
martes, etc. To make the meaning clear, use **el** or **los**
before the days of the week:

el martes = *on Tuesday*   **los martes** = *on Tuesdays*

But you add -s to sábado and domingo
when talking about more than one:

el sábado = *on Saturday*   **los sábados** = *on Saturdays*

In Spanish, the days of the week aren't written
with a capital letter at the beginning.

Red
FOR STOP, THINK,
MAKE A LINK

11 **once** (*on*-se)

12 **doce** (*do*-se)

13 **trece** (*tre*-se)

14 **catorce** (ka-*tor*-se)

15 **quince** (*keen*-se)

+ce

Los números 11–15

The following sentences will help you remember these numbers.

11: **on say**ing this you will remember number 11

12: **do'h say**s Homer Simpson 12 times

13: **tresse**s are curls

14: **cats or ce**nts, what do you prefer?

15: I am very **keen say**s the student. And he repeated it 15 times

Imagination and Association

Invent your own associations for the following numbers if you like. If it's hard to find exactly the same sound in English, use one that is close.

Remember: the Twin Pillars of your language learning are IMAGINATION and ASSOCIATION.

16 **dieciséis** *(dye-see-seys)*

17 **diecisiete** *(dye-see-sye-te)*

18 **dieciocho** *(dye-see-o-cho)*

19 **diecinueve** *(dye-see-nwe-be)*

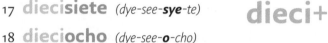

dieci+

los números 16–19

These numbers are constructed in the same way as the English ones, but backwards: **dieciséis** means 10 + 6 (**diez + seis**) and *sixteen* means 6 + 10 ("six-ten").

41

Listen to the numbers 11–29 and practice saying them.

20 **veinte** *(beyn-te)*

21 **veintiuno/una** *(beyn-tee-**oo**-no/**oo**-na)*

22 **veintidós** *(beyn-tee-**dos**)*

23 **veintitrés** *(beyn-tee-**tres**)*

24 **veinticuatro** *(beyn-tee-**kwa**-tro)*

25 **veinticinco** *(beyn-tee-**seen**-ko)*   **veinti+**

26 **veintiséis** *(beyn-tee-**seys**)*

27 **veintisiete** *(beyn-tee-**sye**-te)*

28 **veintiocho** *(beyn-tee-**o**-cho)*

29 **veintinueve** *(beyn-tee-**nwe**-be)*

los números 20-29

If you chose to use the story about Ben and his cat, you could imagine Ben's mother calling him in for his evening meal: "BEN TEA!" She's used to him not listening, so she counts how many times she has to call: "BEN TEA UNO, BEN TEA DÓS, BEN TEA TRÉS …"

Tony's Tip

Have a break

Amazingly, you remember more of what you've learned not immediately after studying it, but a little while later — so take a short break after a study session before starting to revise. After learning all those numbers you may feel like getting up and moving around. If so, go ahead, and then review them before going on.

Nuts & bolts
the 24-hour clock

The 24-hour clock is used more in Mexico than in the US, for opening times (museums, bars), business hours (offices, shops), and visiting hours (hospitals) as well as on bus and train timetables.

You've learned all the numbers you need for the 24 hours. To understand and use the quarter hours, you also need **treinta** (**treyn**-ta) 30 and **cuarenta y cinco** (kwa-**ren**-ta ee **seen**-ko) 45. Here are some examples:

10:00 **diez horas**	09:15 **nueve quince**
22:00 **veintidós horas**	22:30 **veintidós treinta**
14:00 **catorce horas**	02:45 **dos cuarenta y cinco**

42

Read the times below. Then listen and number them in the order in which you hear them.

☐ 09:00 ☐ 16:20 ☐ 04:30

☐ 09:30 ☐ 18:10 ☐ 06:11

☐ 10:25 ☐ 20:05

☐ 13:15 ☐ 23:12

Listen again and practice saying the times.

When is it open?

Michael and John decide to ask the employee in la oficina de turismo about los horarios and the price of las entradas of some museos.

Nuts & bolts
Abre ... Cierra ...

To find out about opening and closing times, ask:
¿Qué horario tiene (el museo)? *(ke o-**ra**-ryo **tye**-ne ...)*

The answer will be something like:
De 9:00 a 20:00 *(de **nwe**-be a **beyn**-te)*
From 9 a.m. to 8 p.m.

and will often include the days of the week as well:
Abre *(a-bre)* **de martes a domingo.**
It's open (literally: It opens) from Tuesday to Sunday.
Cierra *(thye-rra)* **los lunes.**
It's closed (literally: It closes) on Mondays.

Did you know?

Museums

Museums and places of interest are generally closed on one day of the week, so check the opening times when planning your visit. Some, not all, are closed on Mondays. Many of Mexico City's museums offer free admission on Sundays and holidays.

43

Listen to Michael's conversation and note down whether the following statements are *true* verdadero (V) or *false* falso (F). Don't check your answers until you've done the second part of the exercise.

V/F

1. ▢ The Museo Frida Kahlo opens at 10 a.m.
2. ▢ The Museo Frida Kahlo is open from Tuesday to Sunday.
3. ▢ Tickets for the Museo Frida Kahlo cost 20 pesos on Saturdays.
4. ▢ Entry to the Museo Frida Kahlo is free on Sundays.
5. ▢ The Museo Diego Rivera isn't open on Sunday afternoons.
6. ▢ The Museo Diego Rivera is closed on Mondays.
7. ▢ The Museo de Arte Moderno closes at 7 p.m.
8. ▢ The Museo Frida Kahlo and the Museo de Arte Moderno are closed on Mondays.

Listen to the conversation again and complete the table.

	Museo Frida Kahlo	Museo Diego Rivera	Museo de Arte Moderno
Horario			
Horario domingo			
Abre (días)			
Cierra (día)			
Entrada ($)			

go to
www.collinslanguage.com/revolution
for extra activities

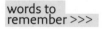

words to
remember >>>

En la taquilla *(en la ta-**kee**-ya)*
At the ticket office

el/la estudiante *(el/la es-too-**dyan**-te)* student

Green
FOR GO AHEAD

Nuts & bolts
man or woman?

Some Spanish words are the same whether they refer to a man or a woman. To make it clear whether a *student* is male or female, you use **el/un** or **la/una**:

el estudiante = *the male student*
una estudiante = *a female student*

Did you know?

A working relationship (2)

A lot of Spanish words begin with **est-**, **esp-**, or **esc-**. If you knock off the e- at the beginning, they often look much more like their English equivalent:

(e)studiante = *student*.

Try it with **estación**, **especial**, and **escultura**

Yellow
FOR WAIT
AND THINK

la puerta *(la **pwair**-ta)* door

la tarifa reducida
*(la ta-**ree**-fa re-doo-**see**-da)* reduced rate

los minusválidos
*(los mee-noos-**ba**-lee-dos)* disabled people

Puerta looks rather like the English words "port" and "portal." Think of a porthole on a ship: not quite a door, but definitely an opening.

Tarifa reducida will remind you of "reduced tariff."

Watch out: **servicios** here means *restroom*, not "services." This is what's known as **un falso amigo**, *a false friend*.

Think about the two words that make up **minusválidos** and find a link to its meaning.

Nuts & bolts
del

You know that **al** = **a** + **el** *(to the, at the)*.
Similarly, **del** = **de** + **el** *(of the)*, so :

al final del pasillo = *at the end of the corridor*

Red

FOR STOP, THINK,
MAKE A LINK

 44

Listen to the green, yellow and red words and practice saying them.

hombres *(om-bres)* men

mujeres *(moo-khair-es)* women

al final del pasillo at the end of the corridor
(al fee-nal del pa-see-lyo)

los baños *(los ba-nyos)* restrooms

Use the power of your imagination to create associations that will help you remember these words.

Mental gymnastics 7

Match the symbols to the words on the signs.

a.

b.

c.

1. ◯ minusválidos

2. ◯ mujeres

3. ◯ hombres

In the museum

John and Michael have decided to visit the Museo Nacional de Antropología.
They find the sign saying TAQUILLA and join the line for entradas. There are several people ahead of them.

Mental gymnastics 8

Read the information below and the conversation.
What kind of ticket does the man buy? How much does it cost?

Asistente museo:	**Buenos días.**
Señor:	**Buenos días. Una entrada, por favor.**
Asistente museo:	**¿Tarifa reducida?**
Señor:	**Sí, por favor.**
Asistente museo:	**Su pasaporte, por favor.**
Señor:	**Aquí tiene.**
Asistente museo:	**Gracias. Son veinte pesos.**

TARIFAS DE ENTRADA AL MUSEO

Entrada general: 30 pesos
Tarifa reducida: 20 pesos
Mayores de 65 años y
estudiantes menores de 25 años previa acreditación

Entrada gratuita: Domingo de 9:00 a 19:00

Mental gymnastics 9

Now read and complete these two conversations.

1. Asistente museo: **Buenas tardes.**

    Señor: **Buenas** ....

    Asistente museo: **¿Entrada general?**

    Señor: .... **¿Cuánto es?**

    Asistente museo: **Treinta pesos.**

    Señor: **Gracias.**

2. Asistente museo: **Buenos días.**

    Estudiante: ....

    Asistente museo: **¿Entrada general?**

    Estudiante: **No, tarifa** ....

    Asistente museo: **Su pasaporte, por favor.**

    Estudiante: **Aquí tiene.**

    Asistente museo: **Gracias. Aquí tiene,
    dos entradas de estudiante.**

John and Michael are inside el museo, but before they start their visit John needs to use the restroom. He looks around for a museum attendant he can ask where los baños are.

Mental gymnastics 10

Can you remember the direction words you learned in Unidad 3? Review them now if you're unsure. Then copy the correct phrase below each symbol.

a la derecha
a la izquierda
todo derecho

1. .... 2. .... 3. ....

Now look at this plan and match the correct phrase to each door.

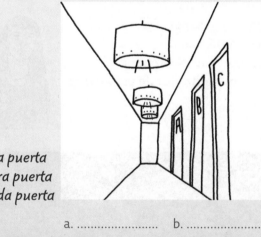

la tercera puerta
la primera puerta
la segunda puerta

a. .... b. .... c. ....

Mental gymnastics 11

Look at the plan, read the directions and write down which restrooms they refer to.

a. **Al final del pasillo a la derecha, la primera puerta a la derecha.** *mujeres*

b. **Al final del pasillo, la primera puerta a la izquierda.** ....

c. **La primera puerta a la izquierda.** ....

d. **Todo derecho. La segunda puerta a la derecha.** ....

e. **Al final del pasillo a la derecha, la tercera puerta a la derecha.** ....

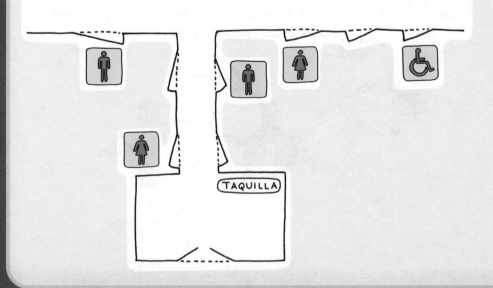

45

Listen to four conversations and match each of them with a set of directions from Mental gymnastics 11.

Conversation 1:

Conversation 2:

Conversation 3:

Conversation 4:

Mind Map it!

In this unit and Unidad 3 you've met a lot of the sort of información you may be given in una oficina de turismo. Our Mind Map shows how you can organize it all clearly, so that it's easy to remember. Add more branches to create your own Mind Map.

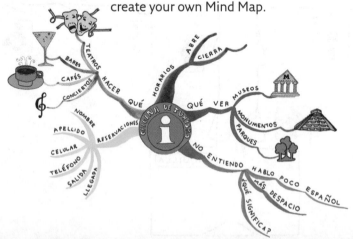

use CD2
for more audio practice and revision

5

De compras

By the end of this unit you will be able to:

- Try on and buy clothes
- Talk about colors and sizes
- Ask where something or somebody is
- Use the numbers 31–199

words to remember >>>

Ropa *(ro-pa)*

Clothes

Green
FOR GO AHEAD

una blusa *(oo-na **bloo**-sa)* a blouse

una chaqueta *(oo-na cha-**ke**-ta)* a jacket

un suéter *(soo**e**-ter)* a sweater

los colores *(los ko-**lo**-res)* the colours

rosa *(**ro**-sa)* pink, rose

naranja *(na-**ran**-kha)* orange

mediano, mediana medium
*(me-**dya**-no, me-**dya**-na)*

Remember to associate the masculine and
feminine words with your strong masculine and feminine
characters.

Yellow

FOR WAIT
AND THINK

 46

Listen to all
these words
and practice
saying them.

un pantalón (a pair of) pants
*(oon pan-ta-**lon**)*

negro, negra (***ne**-gro, **ne**-gra*) black

blanco, blanca (***blan**-ko, **blan**-ka*) white

café (*ka-**feih***) brown

verde (***ber**-de*) green

grande (***gran**-de*) big, large

For **blanco**, think of a blank sheet of white paper with a big O in the middle. You can link **café** with "coffee," which is brown, and **verde** with "verdant," green and lush.

Nuts & bolts
unos and unas

You've already met the words **un** and **una** — *a, an* — used with masculine singular and feminine singular words. We use their plural forms, **unos** and **unas**, — meaning *some* — with masculine plural and feminine plural words.

un suéter = *a sweater*   **unos suéters** = *some sweaters*
una chaqueta = *a jacket*   **unas blusas** = *some blouses*

Mental gymnastics 1

Match the illustrations on the left with the phrases on the right.

1.
2.
3.
4.

a. una blusa verde

b. un suéter rosa

c. un pantalón blanco

d. una chaqueta negra

Nuts & bolts
adding information

Describing words (adjectives) give information about other words, such as color (e.g. **blanco/blanca**) or size (e.g. **grande**).

un suéter blanco = *a white sweater*
una blusa blanca = *a white blouse*

un suéter grande = *a large sweater*
una blusa grande = *a large blouse*

In Spanish, describing words usually go AFTER the word they are describing, whereas in English they usually go before.

check your answers at
www.collinslanguage.com/revolution

Red

FOR STOP, THINK, MAKE A LINK

47

Listen to these words and practice saying them.

un traje *(oon **tra**-khe)* a suit

un vestido *(oon bes-**tee**-do)* a dress

los probadores *(los pro-ba-**do**-res)* the fitting rooms

una camisa *(**oo**-na ka-**mee**-sa)* a shirt

una camiseta *(**oo**-na ka-mee-**se**-ta)* a T-shirt

una falda *(**oo**-na **fal**-da)* a skirt

la talla *(la **ta**-ya)* size

pequeño, pequeña *(pe-**ke**-nyo, pe-**ke**-nya)* small

amarillo, amarilla
*(a-ma-**ree**-yo, a-ma-**ree**-ya)* yellow

rojo, roja *(**ro**-kho, **ro**-kha)* red

gris *(grees)* gray

azul *(a-**sool**)* blue

Watch out: **vestido** looks like "vest," but it's a dress! This is another "false friend."

To remember which word represents which color, link it with an appropriate object: a yellow ARMADILLO, red ROCK, gray GREASE, blue lapis LAZULI (meaning "stone of azure").

You could take this a step further and create a memorable image. For example, picture a yellow armadillo sitting on a yellow submarine and whistling the Beatles' song.

Mental gymnastics 2

Label each segment of the color wheel with the appropriate Spanish word. Check your answers at **www.collinslanguage.com/revolution**

Mental gymnastics 3

Match each white T-shirt with its size in Spanish.

1. ....   2. ....   3. ....

talla grande
talla pequeña
talla mediana

in complete agreement

Describing words always take on the same gender (masculine or feminine) and the same number (singular or plural) as the word they describe. We say they are "in agreement" with it.

- Describing words ending in **-o** change the **-o** to **-a** for the feminine form and add **-s** for the plural:

  un vestido blanco   **una falda blanca**
  unos vestidos blancos   **unas faldas blancas**

- If they end in a vowel other than **-o**, they have the same form in both masculine and feminine and add **-s** for the plural:

  un vestido verde   **una falda verde**
  unos vestidos verdes   **unas faldas verdes**

- If they end in a consonant, they have the same form in both masculine and feminine and add **-es** for the plural:

  un vestido gris   **una falda gris**
  unos vestidos grises   **unas faldas grises**

- Finally, if a masculine and a feminine word share the same describing word, the describing word is in the masculine plural:

  un suéter y una falda blancos = *a white sweater and skirt*

Mental gymnastics 4

Add the appropriate endings to the describing words to complete these descriptions. Note that **rosa** and **naranja** describe the colour of masculine as well as feminine words: their endings never change. You could draw the items to help you remember the phrases.

1. unos vestidos naranj.....
2. una camiseta amarill.....
3. un traje pequeñ.....
4. un pantalón negr.....

Mental gymnastics 5

Look at the pictures and write a description of each item, as in the example.

1. *una camisa azul*

2. ....

3. ....

4. ....

5. ....

48

Listen to these numbers and practice saying them.

30 · **treinta** *(**treyn**-ta)*

31 · **treinta y uno/una** *(**treyn**-ta ee **oo**-no/**oo**-na)*

40 · **cuarenta** *(kwa-**ren**-ta)*

41 · **cuarenta y uno/una**
*(kwa-**ren**-ta ee **oo**-no/**oo**-na)*

43 · **cuarenta y tres** *(kwa-**ren**-ta ee tres)*

50 · **cincuenta** *(seen-**kwen**-ta)*

54 · **cincuenta y cuatro**
*(seen-**kwen**-ta ee **kwa**-tro)*

Los números 30-59

You'll need these numbers to talk about clothes sizes. As you've seen, the numbers 0–30 are written as single words. From 31 onwards, the tens and units are written as separate words linked by **y**.

Nuts & bolts
un, uno, una

Uno is shortened to **un** when it's followed by a masculine word, so we say **número cuarenta y uno** *no. 41* but **cuarenta y un pesos** $41 and **veintiún pantalones**.

Uno is replaced by **una** if it's followed by a feminine word: **treinta y una faldas** *31 skirts*.

Tony's Tip

Use your whole brain!

We all need to use both sides of our brain to maximize our learning abilities. While studying, your left brain is working hard on words, sentences and logic. Your creative right brain kicks into action when you are relaxing — and this is the time to review your visualizations and come up with new ones that work better for you. Involve your right brain by Mind Mapping, drawing pictures, listening to music, and singing songs.

In the department store

After rounding off their visit to el Museo Nacional de Antropología with lunch in the museum's coffee-shop, John and Michael take a stroll in the city center and go into one of la Ciudad de México's big department stores. While they're browsing the men's department, they listen to **la dependienta** *the shop assistant* serving other **clientes** *customers*.

Mental gymnastics 6

Match the questions John and Michael hear with the English equivalents.

¿Tienen (**tye**-nen)
este suéter en la talla ...?

1.

a.
I'd like this skirt
in size ...

Quería (ke-**ree**-a)
esta falda en la talla ...

2.

b.
And in other colors?

Do you have this
sweater in size ...?

¿Y en otra talla?

3.

c.

¿Y en otros colores?

4.

And in another size?

d.

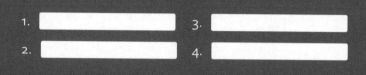

49   Listen to four people asking for clothes in different sizes and write down the size you hear, in both words and figures.

1. ☐   3. ☐

2. ☐   4. ☐

Nuts & bolts
avoiding repetition

When a customer asks **¿Tienen este suéter en la talla ...?**, the assistant answers **Lo siento, pero no lo tenemos**. **Lo** *it* replaces the word **suéter**, to avoid repeating it.

Notice that the Spanish and English words are in a different position in the sentence:

Lo siento, pero no lo tenemos.
I'm sorry, but we don't have it.

Lo, la, los, las — *it* and *them* — agree in number and gender with the word they replace:

	it	them
masculine	lo	los
feminine	la	las

50

Read the **"NUTS & BOLTS"** on avoiding repetition and then complete the short conversations below with the shop assistant's answers. Listen to the conversations on CD1 and practice taking the customer's part.

1. Cliente: **¿Tienen este suéter en la talla grande?**
    Dependienta:

2. Cliente: **¿Tienen este pantalón en la talla cuarenta y seis?**
    Dependienta:
    Cliente: **¿Y en otra talla?**
    Dependienta:

3. Clienta: **¿Tienen estas faldas en color rojo?**
    Dependienta:
    Clienta: **¿Y en otros colores?**
    Dependienta:

Sí, las tenemos en color blanco y en color azul.

Lo siento, pero no las tenemos.

Sí, lo tenemos en la talla cuarenta y cuatro.

Lo siento, pero no lo tenemos.

Sí, un momento por favor. ... Aquí tiene usted.

Mental gymnastics 7

Complete the questions and answers with an appropriate expression from the list.

1. ¿Tienen .... suéter en la talla mediana?
   Lo siento, pero ....

2. ¿Tienen .... faldas en la talla pequeña?
   Lo siento, pero ....

3. Quería .... suéters en la talla grande.
   Lo siento, pero ....

4. Quería .... falda en la talla treinta y dos.
   Lo siento, pero ....

5. ¿Y en .... talla?
   Sí, ...

otra	la tenemos en la talla grande
este	no la tenemos
esta	no los tenemos
estos	no lo tenemos
estas	no las tenemos

Nuts & bolts

this and these

this	*these*
este vestido	**estos** vestidos
esta falda	**estas** faldas

another and other

another	*other*
otro color	**otros** colores
otra talla	**otras** tallas

51

A. Listen to Michael's conversation with la dependienta and answer the questions.

1. What item of clothing does Michael want?

2. In which size?

3. In which color(s)?

B. Listen to the conversation again and tick the phrases you hear.

1. What does Michael ask to find out where the fitting rooms are?

☐ a. ¿Hay probadores?

☐ b. ¿Dónde están los probadores?

☐ c. ¿Dónde está el probador?

2. What does la dependienta answer?

☐ a. Los probadores están allí, a la izquierda.

☐ b. Los probadores están aquí, a la izquierda.

☐ c. Los probadores están ahí, a la derecha.

C. Check your answers and then practice saying Michael's lines along with him.

Nuts & bolts
¿Dónde está(n) ...?

There's no point in asking the shop assistant **¿Hay probadores?**
Are there fitting rooms? because you know there are.
What you need to know is WHERE they are: **dónde están** (*don-*de es-***tan***).

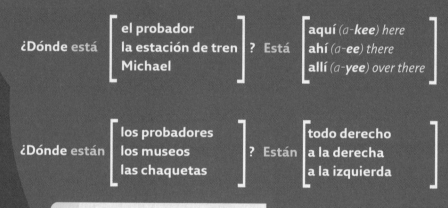

¿Dónde está
el probador
la estación de tren
Michael
? **Está**
aquí (*a-**kee***) here
ahí (*a-**ee***) there
allí (*a-**yee***) over there

¿Dónde están
los probadores
los museos
las chaquetas
? **Están**
todo derecho
a la derecha
a la izquierda

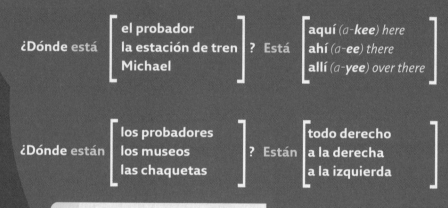

Did you know?

Opening & closing times

To avoid disappointment, always check opening and closing times in the countries you're visiting.

In Mexico most shops are open from 9 or 10 a.m. to 8 p.m., from Monday to Saturday. On Sunday, malls and tourist locations are usually open. Smaller shops usually do not take credit cards; larger stores, especially in tourist centers, can take credit cards but may require you to pay an additional charge.

A good tip when shopping in Mexico is to bargain with the vendors whenever you can. Try negotiating for around half the price they're initially asking you to pay, and you can usually settle for a price somewhere in between.

What a coincidence! Los señores Herbert have just come
into the store. Let's see what they want.

 5²

**Complete the conversation between el dependiente
and la señora Herbert. Then listen and take the place
of la señora Herbert in the conversation. There's a
pause for you to answer before the correct answer
is given.**

Dependiente: **Buenas tardes. ¿En qué les puedo ayudar?**
Señora Herbert:

Do you have this jacket in size 42 in blue?

Dependiente: **Hmm ... Lo siento, pero no la tenemos. En la talla
cuarenta y dos la tenemos en blanco, amarillo y rosa.**

Señora Herbert: **Bueno, pues**

the pink jacket, please.

Dependiente: **Muy bien, aquí tiene usted.**

Señora Herbert:

Where are the fitting rooms?

Dependiente: **Están allí, a la derecha.**

Tony's Tip

Label and remember!

This is an appropriate point to take a break. While you're up
and about, find some sticky notes and label the clothes in
your closet in Spanish.

Remember to include the colors!

**go to
www.collinslanguage.com/revolution
for extra activities**

ciento trece   113

Unit 5

words to remember >>>

Pagar *(pa-gar)*

Paying

el crédito *(el **kre**-dee-to)* credit

el PIN *(el peen)* PIN

Green
FOR GO AHEAD

en efectivo *(en e-fek-**tee**-bo)* in cash

la tarjeta *(la tar-**khe**-ta)* card

con tarjeta de crédito
*(con tar-**khe**-ta de **kre**-dee-to)* by credit card

Red
FOR STOP, THINK,
MAKE A LINK

 53

**Listen to
the green and
red words
and practice
saying them.**

Did you know?

El PIN

Did you know? ... that el PIN in Mexico is also known as firma electronica or electronic signature..

54

Listen to the numbers and practice saying them.

Concentrate on the sound of the words by closing your eyes as you repeat them.

60 **sesenta** *(se-**sen**-ta)*
70 **setenta** *(se-**ten**-ta)*
80 **ochenta** *(o-**chen**-ta)*
90 **noventa** *(no-**ben**-ta)*
100 **cien** *(syen)*
101 **ciento uno/una**
*(**syen**-to **oo**-no/**syen**-to **oo**-na)*
102 **ciento dos** *(**syen**-to dos)*
125 **ciento veinticinco**
*(**syen**-to beyn-tee-**seen**-ko)*
199 **ciento noventa y nueve**
*(**syen**-to no-**ben**-ta ee **nwe**-be)*

Los números 60–199
Note that when **ciento** is NOT followed by another number it's shortened to **cien**: **ciento uno** (101), **ciento treinta** (130), but **cien pesos** (100).

Mental gymnastics 8

Add up these pairs of numbers as quickly as you can and say the sum aloud. Write it in words if that helps you to remember!

a.   83 + 17 =
b.   65 + 73 =
c.   43 + 58 =
d.   99 + 73 =
e.   56 + 62 =

How would you like to pay?

Michael and Mrs Herbert have finished their shopping. They just have to take their purchases to the cash register and pay for them. The first thing the cashier is going to ask is **¿Cómo quiere pagar usted?** – *How do you want to pay?*

🎧 55

Listen to Michael's conversation and answer the questions in English.

1. Which pants does Michael take?

2. Does he pay in cash or by credit card?

3. What document does he have to show?

4. What else does the cashier ask for?

56

**La señora Herbert is at the cash register too.
Listen to her conversation and fill in the gaps.**

Salesclerk **¿Cómo quiere .... usted, con tarjeta
de crédito o ....?**

Harriet Herbert **Con tarjeta de crédito.**

Salesclerk **¿Su tarjeta, ...?**

Harriet Herbert **Aquí tiene usted.**

Salesclerk **Su ...., por favor.**

Harriet Herbert **Aquí tiene.**

Salesclerk **Muy bien. Su ....,
por favor.**

Salesclerk **Muchas gracias.**

Mr & Mrs Herbert **..........................**

57

**Now it's your turn. You've bought a shirt and a pair
of pants and you want to pay by credit card. After
the dependiente speaks, there's a pause for you to
respond, and then you'll hear the correct answer.**

Mind Map it!

Add all the shopping words you know to the Mind Map.

use CD2
for more audio practice and revision

6

En el restaurante

By the end of this unit you will be able to:

- Ask for a table in a restaurant
- Order a meal and drinks
- Use the numbers 200-999
- Read a travel brochure in Spanish

words to
remember >>>

El menú del día *(el me-noo del dee-a)*
Today's menu

First, let's revise some words you already know from
Unidad 1 and Unidad 3. They'll be useful when ordering a
meal in a restaurant.

Mental gymnastics 1

Copy these words for food and drinks under the headings **para comer** and
para beber, to make a café menu. Add **el**, **la**, **los**, or **las** in front of each word to
show whether it's masculine or feminine.

Coca-Cola   jugo de naranja
                 refresco

          botella **de** agua mineral   queso
refresco

     vino   pan   café **con** leche

          té **con** limón   cervezas
tacos   café **negro**
          tortilla   camarones

     fruta   leche

Café Paraíso, Cancún

PARA BEBER   PARA COMER

Green
FOR GO AHEAD

un tequila *(oon te-**kee**-la)* tequila

un flan *(**oon** flan)* flan

una sopa *(**oo**-na **so**-pa)* soup

una ensalada *(**oo**-na en-sa-**la**-da)* salad

Yellow
FOR WAIT
AND THINK

el primer plato *(el pree-**mair pla**-to)* first course

el segundo plato
*(el se-**goon**-do **pla**-to)* second course

el vino blanco/tinto
*(el **bee**-no **blan**-ko/**teen**-to)* white/red wine

el atún *(el a-**toon**)* tuna

el bistec *(el bees-**tek**)* steak

la carne *(la **kar**-ne)* meat

You know **primero** and **segundo**, and **plato** looks like
"plate," so you can easily work out the meaning of **primer
plato** and **segundo plato**. *White wine*, **vino blanco**, is
straightforward, but *red wine* in Spanish is **tinto** — "tinted."
Bistec is a Spanish word borrowed from English: "beef steak"!
Atún uses the same letters as *tuna* in a different order. For
carne think of "carnivore," someone who eats meat.

Red
FOR STOP, THINK,
MAKE A LINK

 58

Listen to the green, yellow and red words and practice saying them.

el postre *(el **pos**-tre)* dessert

el arroz *(el a-**rroth**)* rice

el pescado *(el pes-**ka**-do)* fish

el pollo *(el **po**-yo)* chicken

la nieve *(la nee-**ay**-be)* ice cream

la comida *(la ko-**mee**-da)* food, lunch

la mesa *(la **me**-sa)* table

la ternera *(la tair-**ne**-ra)* veal

frito, frita *(**free**-to, **free**-ta)* fried

a la plancha *(a la **plan**-cha)* grilled

Make associations to help you remember these words. Here are some suggestions to start you off.

Arroz *rice*: an ARROw with a "S" on its arrowhead stuck into a bag of rice.

Postre *dessert*: to remember this word think of having your **postre**, POST main course.
Mesa *table*: "Don't MESS Around, set the table at once!"

Now it's over to you to create your own images.
Let your imagination run wild!

Mental gymnastics 2

Match the pictures to the Spanish words.

1. pollo
2. una mesa
3. el postre
4. arroz
5. pescado
6. una nieve

a

b

c

d

e

f

Did you know?

La comida

In Latin America and Spain, the main meal of the day is lunch, **la comida**, which usually consists of several courses: **primer plato**, **segundo plato**, **postre**, and **café**.

Many eating places offer a fixed-price menu, **la comida corrida**, or **el menú del día** which is generally cheaper than eating à la carte, **comer a la carta**.

A table, please!

Do you remember la señora Velvet enjoying her vino and botanas in Unidad 1? It's now 2 p.m. and she's ready for la comida. She goes into a popular restaurante at the beautiful beach resort in Cancún, Mexico, where she's staying, and asks for a table: **Una mesa, por favor**.

¡Buen provecho!

As la señora Velvet sits down, she says **¡Buen provecho!**
(boo-**en** pro-**be**-cho) *Enjoy your meal!* to the people at the nearby tables.

59 **Listen to the conversation and practice asking for a table.**

60 **Listen to two more conversations and note down how many people want to have lunch.**

1. una mesa para
2. una mesa para

Nuts & bolts
al ..., a la ...

On a menu, **al** or **a la** often indicates the style of a dish or the way it's cooked:

a la mexicana *mexican style*   **a la plancha** *grilled*
al horno *baked*   **al vapor** *steamed*

Remember that **al** is **a** + **el**.

¡Buen provecho!

Did you know?

It's polite to say **¡Buen provecho!** when entering a place where there are people eating, and before beginning a meal with others.

The usual response is **¡Gracias!**

La señora Velvet sits down and el mesero brings her
la carta, *the menu*. She looks at el menú del día.

Mental gymnastics 3

Match the Mexican dishes with the English descriptions.

1. **Arroz con leche**

2. **Atún a la plancha**

3. **Camarones fritos**

4. **Bistec a la plancha**

5. **Enchiladas de pollo**

6. **Ensalada azteca**

7. **Fajitas de ternera**

8. **Flan**

9. **Fruta**

10. **Guacamole con nachos**

11. **Nieve**

12. **Pescado del día**

13. **Sopa de tortilla**

a. *Lettuce, deep-fried tortilla strips, tomatoes, and fresh cheese, tossed with chilli and chilli oil*

b. *Avocado soup with fresh local cheese, crispy tortilla strips, slivers of chilli pepper, and sour cream*

c. *Rice pudding*

d. *Grilled steak*

e. *Catch of the day*

f. *Fruit*

g. *Ice cream*

h. *Grilled tuna*

i. *Fried shrimp*

j. *Tender strips of chicken breast with sweet peppers and onions*

k. *Flan*

l. *A folded tortilla filled with a seasoned veal mixture and covered with chilli sauce*

m. *Mashed avocado with tomato, onion, and spices, served with tortilla chips*

Mental gymnastics 4

Look at the dishes in Mental gymnastics 3 again and sort them under these headings. (You will have three dishes left over!)

Carne

....
....
....
....
....

Pescado

....
....
....
....
....

Postre

....
....
....
....
....

61

Listen to la señora Velvet ordering la comida and write down what she orders.

Primer plato:

Segundo plato:

Bebida:

Postre:

62

Now it's your turn to order. Read the conversation below and fill in your lines in Spanish (or go straight to the CD and write them down as you listen). Then listen to the conversation and act it out.

Camarero: **Sí, dígame.**

Usted: **De primer plato** ⬜⬜⬜⬜ **y de segundo**

⬜⬜⬜⬜

For the first course, tortilla soup, and for the second, catch of the day.

Camarero: **¿Algo de beber?**

Usted: ⬜⬜⬜⬜

White wine, please.

Camarero: **¿Algo de postre?**

Usted: ⬜⬜⬜⬜

A flan, please.

Camarero: **¿Café?**

Usted: ⬜⬜⬜⬜ *No, thank you.*

Tony's Tip

Good news for tactile learners

Everyone's a tactile learner when it comes to eating!

You'll learn food vocabulary best by practicing while eating — so live it up a little! Go to your local Mexican restaurant or prepare your own dishes. It's the perfect opportunity to practice saying your new words while doing something physical — eating and drinking!

Mind Map it!

Complete the Mind Map with the dishes
you've seen in this unit.

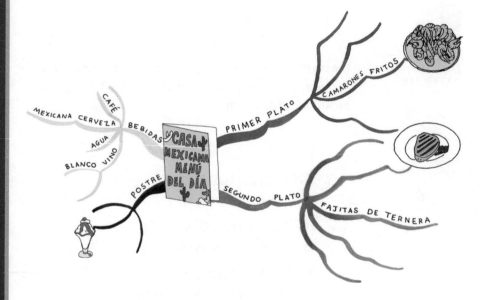

go to
www.collinslanguage.com/revolution
for extra activities

ciento veintinueve 129

words to remember >>>

Un folleto *(oon fo-**ye**-to)*

A brochure

Red
FOR STOP, THINK,
MAKE A LINK

la cocina *(la ko-**see**-na)* cuisine, cooking, kitchen

la playa *(la **pla**-ya)* beach

Create images that will help you remember these words. For example, for **la playa** think of children PLAYing on a beautiful sandy beach.

 63

Listen to the red words and practice saying them.

200 **DOScientos/as**
*(dos-**syen**-tos / dos-**syen**-tas)*

300 **TREScientos/as**
*(tres-**syen**-tos / tres-**syen**-tas)*

 64

Listen to the numbers and practice saying them.

400 **CUATROcientos/as**
*(kwa-tro-**syen**-tos / kwa-tro-**syen**-tas)*

500 **QUINientos/as**
*(keen-**yen**-tos / keen-**yen**-tas)*

600 **SEIScientos/as**
*(seys-**syen**-tos / seys-**syen**-tas)*

700 **SETEcientos/as**
*(se-te-**syen**-tos / se-te-**syen**-tas*

800 **OCHOcientos/as**
*(o-cho-**syen**-tos / o-cho-**syen**-tas)*

900 **NOVEcientos/as**
*(no-be-**syen**-tos / no-be-**syen**-tas)*

Los números 200-999

The numbers 500, 700 and 900 aren't quite what you might expect. Look at them carefully.

Remember: to form the numbers in between, you just add tens and units to the hundreds:

203 **doscientos/as tres**
325 **trescientos/as veinticinco**

Nuts & bolts

Hundreds have the same gender as the word that follows them:

doscientos jugos
but
doscientas cervezas

65 **Listen and copy out the numbers in the order in which you hear them. (They aren't recorded in numerical order.) Then practice reading them aloud in Spanish.**

500	543	777	987	451	908
212	690	311	507	743	821

66 **You'll hear four numbers in English. After each one there's a pause for you to say the number in Spanish and then you'll hear the correct answer.**

Mental gymnastics 5

What a party! Match each number with an appropriate word. (Several combinations are possible.) Then rewrite the numbers in figures and check your answers.

doscientas
cuatrocientos veintiséis
trescientos noventa y tres
quinientas cincuenta
ochocientas cuarenta y cuatro

ensaladas
flanes
sopas
tequilas
tortillas

Reading about Cancún

While she drinks her café, la señora Velvet is reading un folleto about Cancún.

CANCÚN – MÉXICO

Cancún es un destino turístico muy importante. Está en la región de la península de Yucatán. Su clima es semi-tropical: tiene una temperatura típica de 80° F, pero puede llegar a los 95° F durante el verano, con días soleados durante la mayor parte del año.

Bañado por las aguas turquesa del mar Caribe, Cancún ofrece la increíble belleza de sus playas en las que se puede practicar todo tipo de actividades y deportes acuáticos, tomar el sol o bien disfrutar los servicios y comodidades que ofrece su impresionante zona hotelera, de más de 30 km de extensión, donde hay hoteles de cinco estrellas, exclusivos resorts y spas, modernos centros comerciales, más de 500 restaurantes que ofrecen una cocina nacional e internacional extraordinaria, y numerosos bares y discos.

Cerca de Cancún están Playa del Carmen, Xcaret y Xel-Há, antiguos puertos mayas, hoy convertidos en paraísos ecoturísticos; y la interesante zona arqueológica de Tulum, una ciudad de la cultura maya. Cerca de Cancún, a varios kilómetros de la costa, están Isla Mujeres y Cozumel, islas ideales para la práctica del esnórquel.

Mental gymnastics 6

Read el folleto and don't worry if you can't understand every single word. Bearing in mind that you are reading about a tourist resort, see how much of the meaning you can guess. If you read the text two or three times, you'll probably be able to work out a little more each time.

Tony's Tip

Understanding what you read

Before starting to read a text, think about its subject. Read the text right through, without stopping at unfamiliar words. Then read it again, underlining the words and expressions you don't understand. Look at where these words appear and guess their meaning, using the words around them as clues.

For example, in the Cancún brochure, if you've underlined the words **Bañado**, **turquesa**, and **mar** in **Bañado por las aguas turquesa del mar Caribe**, first think about **aguas**: the waters of what? Look for another word to give you a clue: **Caribe** is similar to *Caribbean*, and you know the Caribbean is a sea, so **aguas ... del mar Caribe** can only be *waters of the Caribbean Sea*. **Turquesa** looks like *turquoise* and in this context it must refer to the color of the water.

Finally, what about the word **bañado**? It looks very like **baño** *bath*. So Cancún *is bathed by the turquoise waters of the Caribbean Sea*.

Mental gymnastics 7

Find the Spanish equivalents of the following in el folleto.

1. five-star hotels
2. sunny days
3. sunbathe
4. during the summer
5. most of the year
6. take advantage of the services and facilities
7. the incredible beauty of its beaches

Mental gymnastics 8

Read el folleto again and decide whether these statements are
true **verdadero (V)** or *false* **falso (F)**. Correct the false statements.

V/F

1. ☐ The average temperature in Cancún is 95° F.

2. ☐ Summer is the hottest season of the year.

3. ☐ Cancún has rain on most days of the year.

4. ☐ In Cancún one can sunbathe.

5. ☐ Tulum is a city of the Mayan civilization.

6. ☐ Isla Mujeres and Cozumel are a few kilometres off the coast.

La señora Velvet has finished her comida and wants
to pay and go back to her hotel for **una siesta**.
Can you remember how to ask for the check? If you aren't
sure, look back at Unidad 1.

◎ 67

**Listen to la señora Velvet and two other diners asking
for la cuenta. Note down how much each meal costs.**

Conversation 1: ⬜

Conversation 2: ⬜

Conversation 3: ⬜

**You could add a branch for la cuenta, números, and
pesos to your Mind Map for Unidad 6.**

Did you know?

A working relationship (3)

There are thousands of Spanish and English words that are
spelled in exactly or almost exactly the same way and
have the same or a similar meaning in both languages.
You'll recognize them immediately in print, but the
Spanish pronunciation is almost always a little different.

Here are some "working relationships" between English
and Spanish. Compare the following pairs of words:

exclusive = **exclusivo**   *incredible* = **increíble**
positive = **positivo**   *notable* = **notable**

Can you work out the Spanish for these English words?
*negative, creative, primitive, superlative, motive
horrible, probable, irresistible, adorable, inexplicable*

use CD2
for more audio practice and revision

7

De excursión

By the end of this unit you will be able to:

- Ask about departure and arrival times
- Buy bus and train tickets
- Use and understand the 12-hour clock
- Express likes and dislikes
- Predict the Spanish equivalents
  of hundreds of English words

¿A qué hora ...? *(a ke o-ra)*

At what time ...?

Green
FOR GO AHEAD

cuarto para *(kwar-to pa-ra)* quarter to

diez para *(dyes pa-ra)* ten to

y cuarto *(ee kwar-to)* quarter past

y diez *(ee dyeth)* ten past

Yellow
FOR WAIT
AND THINK

en punto *(en poon-to)* exactly

y media *(ee me-dya)* half past

cada media hora
(ka-da me-dya o-ra) every half hour

To remember **en punto**, think of it as an exact point in time.

Media, *half*, is similar to **mediano**, *medium*, which you met in Unidad 5.

Cada means *each* or *every*. It always ends in **-a**.

Red

FOR STOP, THINK,
MAKE A LINK

 68

Listen to the
green, yellow
and red words
and practice
saying them.

de la mañana *(de la ma-nya-na)* in the morning

de la tarde *(de la tar-de)* in the afternoon

de la noche *(de la no-che)* in the evening, at night

un boleto *(un bo-le-to)* a ticket

de ida *(de ee-da)* one-way

de ida y vuelta *(de ee-da ee bwel-ta)* round-trip

sale *(sa-le)* it leaves

llega *(ye-ga)* it arrives

Use **un boleto** for public transport tickets. Remember that an entrance ticket for a museum, theater, etc. is **una entrada**.

To help you remember **boleto**, imagine a Mexican woman getting ready for a BALL putting on red stiLETTO shoes: one stiletto has a bus ticket stuck on it.

An image you could use for **de la noche** is a sign in the park saying "NO CHEss after 8 p.m." — but remember, the most effective associations are the ones you make yourself.

Mental gymnastics 1

Ask for these train tickets. First say the phrases and then write them down.

1. a one-way ticket to Guadalajara *Un boleto de ida para Guadalajara, por favor.*

2. a round-trip ticket to Acapulco ....

3. a round-trip ticket to Oaxaca ....

4. a one-way ticket to Veracruz ....

◎ 69

Read the "NUTS & BOLTS" opposite. Listen to the times and check the ones you hear. Then practice saying the times aloud in Spanish. You could also write them down.

a. ☐ 8:00 a.m.   e. ☐ 5:15 p.m.

b. ☐ 11:30 p.m.   f. ☐ 4:20 p.m.

c. ☐ 1:25 p.m.   g. ☐ 3:35 a.m.

d. ☐ 5:15 a.m.   h. ☐ 10:30 p.m.

Did you know?

Talking about timetables

Bus and train timetables and station announcements use the 24-hour clock, but the person behind the counter will often use the 12-hour clock when talking about departure and arrival times.

check your answers at
www.collinslanguage.com/revolution

Nuts & bolts
the 12-hour clock

en punto

cinco **para**   **y** cinco

diez **para**   **y** diez

cuarto **para**   **y** cuarto

veinte **para**   **y** veinte

veinticinco **para**   **y** veinticinco

y media

- **La** or **las** is used before the hour: **la una** but **las dos**, **las tres ...**

- The hour is given first, then the minutes:
  las seis y veinte = *six twenty*
  But **cinco para las ocho** = *five to eight*

- Times on the hour are often followed by **en punto**:
  las nueve en punto = *nine o'clock exactly*

Nuts & bolts
a.m. and p.m.

From midnight to noon: **de la mañana**
1:30 a.m. = **la una y media de la mañana**

From noon to nightfall: **de la tarde**
1:30 p.m. = **la una y media de la tarde**

From nightfall to midnight: **de la noche**
10:10 p.m. = **las diez y diez de la noche**

Let's take the bus

La señora Velvet, Rose, has met another guest at her hotel in Cancún. Mary Fisher is also from the United States and like Rose is travelling around **México**. They get on really well and have decided to go on an excursion together. Over a drink, they're reading about some of the places to see around Cancún.

Mental gymnastics 2

Read el folleto about places of interest **cerca de Cancún**, *near Cancún*, and see how much you can understand.

Underline the words in the folleto that are the same or nearly the same in English. Then find these Spanish words in the text and match them to their English equivalents.

1. largo   a. *World Heritage Site*

2. ancho   b. *several*

3. lugar   c. *place*

4. varias   d. *long*

5. Patrimonio de la Humanidad   e. *wide*

Check your answers and then read el folleto again.
How much more can you understand?

SITIOS PARA VISITAR CERCA DE CANCÚN

Isla Mujeres

Isla Mujeres, a 10 kilómetros de Cancún en ferry, es una isla de 8 kilómetros de largo por 800 metros de ancho. Su playa más famosa es "Playa de los Cocos" que, con sus aguas tranquilas, es un lugar perfecto para la práctica de deportes acuáticos.

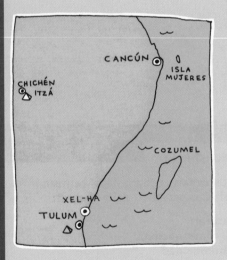

Playa del Carmen

Es un pueblo de ambiente vibrante, localizado a 68 kilómetros de Cancún. Su calle principal, la Quinta Avenida, tiene muchos restaurantes al aire libre, bares, tiendas de artesanías y hoteles.

Xel-Ha

Para los antiguos mayas, su nombre significa "Sitio donde nace el agua". Situado a 115 kilómetros de Cancún, este acuario natural es considerado el más grande del mundo. Está formado por varias lagunas.

Chichén Itzá

Chichén Itzá, a 200 kilómetros de Cancún, está considerado como Patrimonio de la Humanidad y es una de las siete maravillas del mundo. Este magnífico complejo maya es uno de los más grandes en México. En el centro está la majestuosa pirámide de Kukulkán.

Mental gymnastics 3

According to the folleto, where could Rose and Mary do the following?

1. see one of the Seven Wonders of the World ....

2. shop for souvenirs ....

3. enjoy water sports ....

4. visit the biggest natural aquarium
   in the world ....

5. have a good night out ....

6. explore one of the biggest Mayan sites ....

7. take a boat to an island ....

8. see a pyramid ....

Did you know?

A working relationship (4)

Here are some more "working relationships" between English and Spanish. Compare these pairs of words:

> *natural* = **natural**
> *international* = **internacional**
> *humanity* = **humanidad**
> *tranquillity* = **tranquilidad**
> *vibrant* = **vibrante**
> *stimulating* = **estimulante**

Can you work out the Spanish for these English words?
principal, normal, general, nationality, university, diversity, constant, important, elegant.

Rose and Mary decide to spend the day in Playa del Carmen. One of the best ways to travel in México is by autobús, also called **camión**, so they head for **la estación de autobuses** (or **la estación de camiones**) to find out about **el horario de autobuses**, *the bus timetable*, and how much **los boletos** cost.

Nuts & bolts
¿A qué hora ...?

To find out when there is a bus/train:
- **¿A qué hora hay un autobús/hay autobuses para la Ciudad de México?**
- **Cada diez minutos/Cada media hora/Cada hora.**
  Every ten minutes/Every half hour/Every hour.

To find out at what time the bus/train leaves:
- **¿A qué hora sale el autobús para Cancún?**
- **A la una de la tarde/A las once de la mañana.**

To find out at what time the bus/train arrives:
- **¿A qué hora llega el tren a Colima?**
- **A la una de la tarde/A las nueve de la mañana.**

Mental gymnastics 4

A. Using the phrases in the "NUTS & BOLTS" on page 145, can you work out how to ask these questions in Spanish?

1. What time is there a train to Guadalajara?

   ....

2. What time does the bus to Acapulco leave?

   ....

3. What time are there buses to Cancún?

   ....

4. What time does the train arrive in la Ciudad de México?

   ....

B. Now translate the ticket clerk's answers into English.

1. A las diez y diez de la mañana.

   ....

2. Sale al cuarto para las cinco de la tarde.

   ....

3. Cada media hora.

   ....

4. Llega a las nueve y cuarto de la noche.

   ....

Mental gymnastics 5

Look at the departure and arrival times of the buses from Cancún to Playa del Carmen and give yourself 60 seconds to complete the sentences, using the 12-hour clock and writing out the times in words. Then practice saying them aloud.

	Cancún SALIDA	Playa del Carmen LLEGADA
1.	10:15	11:35
2.	11:00	12:20
3.	11:40	13:00
4.	12:30	13:45
5.	13:10	14:30

1. El autobús sale a las ....._diez y cuarto_..... de la _mañana_........ y
   llega al ....._veinticinco para las doce_... de la ...._mañana_..... .

2. El autobús sale a las .... en punto de la .... y
   llega a las .... de la ....

3. El autobús sale al .... de la .... y
   llega a la .... de la ....

4. El autobús sale ....
   ....

5. El autobús ....
   ....

70

Listen to two people asking about bus times at the estación de autobuses de Cancún. Choose the correct answers below.

Conversation 1

1. What time is there a bus to Mérida?

    a. ☐ 9:10 p.m.   b. ☐ 10:00 a.m.   c. ☐ 8:50 a.m.

2. What time does it arrive?

    a. ☐ 2:00 p.m.   b. ☐ 10:20 a.m.   c. ☐ 10:10 p.m.

Conversation 2

1. What time does the bus to Tulum leave?

    a. ☐ 1:30 p.m.   b. ☐ 12:30 p.m.   c. ☐ 9:30 a.m.

2. What time does it arrive?

    a. ☐ 2:45 p.m.   b. ☐ 1:45 p.m.   c. ☐ 11:15 a.m.

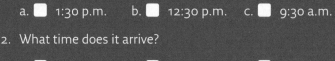 71

Now listen to the two people buying boletos and note the details in the table, using figures.

	Type of ticket	Price per ticket	Number of tickets	Total price
Conversation 1				
Conversation 2				

Complete the conversation between Mary
and the ticket clerk, en la estación de autobuses de
Cancún. Then listen and practice taking Mary's part
in the conversation. There's a pause for you to
answer and then you'll hear the correct answer.

Boletero: **Buenos días.**
Mary: _____

*Good morning. What time are there buses to
Playa del Carmen?*

Boletero: **¿Para Playa del Carmen? Cada hora. Hay uno a las
once de la mañana.**
Mary: _____

What time does it arrive?

Boletero: **A las doce y veinte de la tarde.**
Mary: _____

How much does a round-trip ticket cost?

Boletero: **Setenta y cinco pesos.**
Mary: _____

Two round-trip tickets, please.

Boletero: **Aquí tiene, son ciento cincuenta pesos.**

Mind Map it!

Our Mind Map shows how you can combine what you learned in Unidad 4 about opening and closing times with the new phrases in this unit about bus and train times. Add the missing words and more branches to create your own Mind Map.

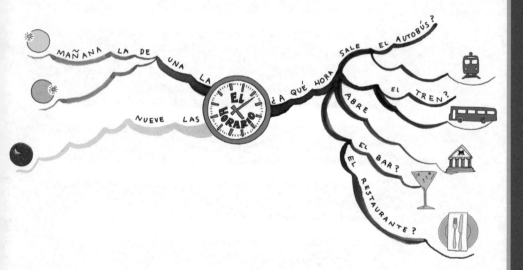

MAÑANA LA DE UNA LA
NUEVE LAS
EL HORARIO
¿A QUÉ HORA SALE EL AUTOBÚS?
EL TREN?
ABRE
EL BAR?
EL RESTAURANTE?

go to
www.collinslanguage.com/revolution
for extra activities

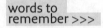

words to
remember >>>

En el mercado *(en el mair-ka-do)*

In the market

Yellow
FOR WAIT
AND THINK

probar *(pro-bar)* to try on

un sombrero *(un som-bre-ro)* a hat

To remember **probar**, think of "probing" something to test it and "prove" that it's good.

Un sombrero is the general word for *a hat*, not necessarily a big Mexican sombrero.

Red
FOR STOP, THINK,
MAKE A LINK

de acuerdo *(de a-ku-er-do)* OK

me gusta *(me goos-ta)* I like (it)

me queda bien *(me ke-da byen)* it fits me

me lo llevo *(me lo lye-bo)* I'll take it

 73

**Listen to the
yellow and
red words
and practice
saying them.**

Make up your own associations and images to help you remember these phrases.

Nuts & bolts
likes and dislikes

To say that you like or dislike something, you use **(no) me gusta** or **(no) me gustan**. These expressions agree with what is liked, not with who does the liking: **(no) me gusta** — literally: *it pleases (doesn't please) me* — goes with singular words and **(no) me gustan** — literally: *they please (don't please) me* goes with plural words.

(No) me gusta {
el sombrero
la chaqueta
el tequila
}

(No) me gustan {
los insectos
las faldas
los trenes
}

Mental gymnastics 6

Read the "NUTS & BOLTS" and then complete the sentences, as in the examples.

🙂   🙁

¡ *Me gusta* .... el pescado!   ¡...................... la falda!

¡ .... el pantalón verde!   ¡ *No me gustan* los autobuses!

¡...................... México!   ¡...................... los sombreros rojos!

¡...................... el español!   ¡...................... la nieve de naranja!

I'll take it!

Rose and Mary are happily browsing around the amazing open-air mercado in Playa del Carmen. Mary spots some attractive sombreros on one of the stalls, so they stop for a closer look. Will she find one that fits?

Mental gymnastics 7

Match the Spanish shopping phrases with their English equivalents.

1. De acuerdo, me lo llevo.
2. Me queda pequeño.
3. No me gusta.
4. ¿Puedo probar ...?
5. Me queda bien.
6. ¿Cuánto es?

a. *It's too small.*
b. *Can I try ...?*
c. *It fits.*
d. *I don't like it.*
e. *How much is it?*
f. *OK, I'll take it.*

Nuts & bolts
I'll take it!

Remember that **lo, la, los, las** — *it* and *them* — agree in number and gender with the word they replace, so *I'll take it/them* = **Me lo/la/los/las llevo**.

Mental gymnastics 8

How would you say the following in Spanish? Read the "NUTS & BOLTS" and then write your answers.

1. *The hat is too big.* ....

2. *The hat is too small.* ....

3. *The hat fits.* ....

4. *Can I try the red hat?* ....

5. *I'll take it* (el sombrero). ....

6. *I'll take it* (la blusa). ....

7. *I'll take it* (el pantalón). ....

Tony's Tip

Body language

Your face and body are just as eloquent as your words.
Smile with your eyes, gesture with your hands!

Nuts & bolts
too big, too small, it fits!

One thing:

(El sombrero)
(La chaqueta) } me queda { grande
pequeño/a
bien

More than one thing:

(Los sombreros)
(Las chaquetas) } me quedan { grandes
pequeños/as
bien

 74

Listen to the conversation between Mary and the stallholder, un hombre mexicano, *a Mexican man.* **Check what you hear.**

	me gusta	no me gusta	me gustan	no me gustan
El sombrero rojo y el sombrero azul	☐	☐	☐	☐
El sombrero amarillo	☐	☐	☐	☐

75

Rose is also trying on some hats. Using the phrases below, complete her conversation with el hombre mexicano. Then listen and practice taking Rose's part in the conversation. There's a pause for you to answer and then you'll hear the correct answer.

- *De acuerdo, me lo llevo.*
- *Me queda pequeño. ¿Lo tiene en otra talla?*
- *El rojo no me gusta. ¿Puedo probarme el sombrero azul?*
- *Hmm, me queda bien, me gusta. ¿Cuánto es?*
- *¡Doscientos pesos! Ciento veinticinco pesos y me lo llevo.*
- *Un sombrero.*

Hombre:	**Y usted, señora. ¿Un sombrero, un vestido, un traje ...?**
Rose:	
Hombre:	**¡Mire el rojo qué bonito!**
Rose:	
Hombre:	**Sí, aquí tiene.**
Rose:	
Hombre:	**En azul no. Tengo un sombrero verde en la talla mediana.**
Rose:	
Hombre:	**Son doscientos pesos**.
Rose:	
Hombre:	**Ciento cincuenta.**
Rose:	

use CD2
for more audio practice and revision

8

¡Qué calor!

By the end of this unit you will be able to:

- Talk about the weather
- Introduce yourself and other people
- Ask people about themselves
- Buy food in a market

words to
remember >>>

El tiempo *(el **tyem**-po)*
The weather

Green
FOR GO AHEAD

76

Listen to
these words
and practice
saying them.

la temperatura
*(la tem-pe-ra-**too**-ra)* the temperature

grados *(**gra**-dos)* degrees (°F)

bajo cero *(**ba**-kho **se**-ro)* below zero

hace fresco *(**a**-se **fres**-ko)* it's fresh

el norte *(el **nor**-te)* the north

el sur *(el soor)* the south

el este *(el **es**-te)* the east

el oeste *(el o-**es**-te)* the west

el centro *(el **sen**-tro)* the center

77

**Say these temperatures aloud. You may want
to write them down. Then listen to check and
practice saying them.**

a. 90°F   b. 75°F   c. 14°F   d. −5°F

e. 45°F   f. 65°F   g. 40°F   h. 104°F

hace ... calor *(ka-lor)* it's warm/hot

frío *(**free**-o)* it's cold

viento *(**byen**-to)* it's windy

sol *(sol)* it's sunny

Link **(hace) calor** with "calorific energy" or Calor gas. **(hace) frío** is similar to "freeze." For **(hace) viento** picture a ventilator blowing air, and you can link **(hace) sol** with "solar energy."

hoy *(oy)* today

llueve *(**yooe**-be)* it's raining

nieva *(**nye**-ba)* it's snowing

hay nubes *(aee **noo**-bes)* it's cloudy

hace ... *(**a**-se)*

 78

buen tiempo *(bwen **tyem**-po)* the weather is good

mal tiempo *(mal **tyem**-po)* the weather is bad

Use your imagination to create your own images and associations for these words.

For example, for **nubes** imagine three NEW BEES buzzing around in the clouds in a cloudy day. Alternatively, think of the related English word "nebulous."

Nuts & bolts
the weather

To ask what the weather is like, you say: **¿Qué tiempo hace?**

The answer will probably be an expression with **hace**:
Hace calor/frío/fresco.
Hace viento/sol.
Hace buen/mal tiempo.

Exceptions are:
Hay nubes. Llueve. Nieva.

To ask about the temperature, you say:
¿Qué temperatura hace? *What is the temperature?*

The answer will be something like:
(Hace) cuarenta grados. (40° F)
(Hace) cinco grados bajo cero. (−5° F)

Mental gymnastics 1

Look at the weather symbols and answer the question.

¿Qué tiempo hace?

1. ....

2. ....

3. ....

4. ....

5. ....

6. ....

7. ....

8. ....

9. ....

Nuts & bolts
commenting on the weather

	calor!	*Isn't it hot!*
	frío!	*Isn't it cold!*
¡Qué	**viento!**	*Isn't it windy!*
	buen tiempo!	*What lovely weather!*
	mal tiempo!	*What terrible weather!*

79   **Listen to the expressions in the
"NUTS & BOLTS" and practice repeating them.**

Mind Map it!

Complete the weather Mind Map using the words you've just learned.

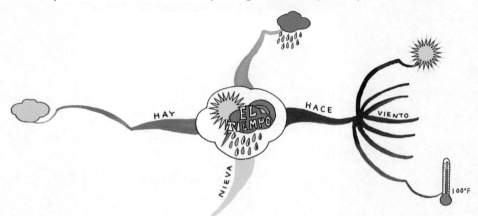

Small talk

Who doesn't talk about el tiempo? Hace buen tiempo: everybody seems happier; hace mal tiempo: the perfect excuse for a moan. Even complete strangers on a bus or train will start chatting about it. So being able to talk about el tiempo in Spanish could help you to get to know people — before you know it, you'll be telling them about yourself!

 80

Look at the map of Mexico and listen to the information about today's weather. Complete the sentences below.

1. En el norte de México hoy

2. En el sur

3. En el este

4. En el oeste

Mental gymnastics 2

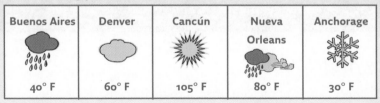

Buenos Aires	Denver	Cancún	Nueva Orleans	Anchorage
40° F	60° F	105° F	80° F	30° F

1. *En Buenos Aires hace mal tiempo: llueve y hace frío. Hace cuarenta grados.*

2. ....

3. ....

4. ....

5. ....

Mental gymnastics 3

1. When talking to people, sometimes you will need to make them aware that you don't understand, so let's revise the phrases you learned in Unidad 4. What would you say in Spanish in these situations?

   a. You don't understand.
   b. You want to explain that you don't speak much Spanish.
   c. Somebody is talking too fast for you.
   d. You don't know the meaning of the word **vacaciones**.

2. If somebody says **No entiendo, ¿puede repetir, por favor?**, what do you think you are being asked to do?

81   **Listen to check your answers to**
Mental gymnastics 3 and repeat the phrases.

Mental gymnastics 4

Match the Spanish names of the countries with their English equivalents.

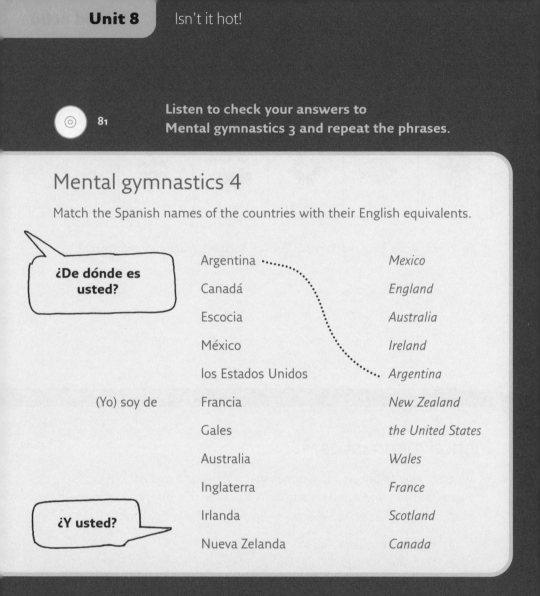

¿De dónde es usted?

Argentina	Mexico
Canadá	England
Escocia	Australia
México	Ireland
los Estados Unidos	Argentina
(Yo) soy de Francia	New Zealand
Gales	the United States
Australia	Wales
Inglaterra	France
Irlanda	Scotland
Nueva Zelanda	Canada

¿Y usted?

El fin de semana is over. Michael and John are back at work, Pablo and Cristina have gone home, Rose Velvet and Mary Fisher are visiting Chichén Itzá and los señores Herbert are planning to leave la Ciudad de México and travel towards el sur for a few days in **Acapulco**.

Harriet Herbert is waiting in the hotel lobby for su esposo and looking at *the weather section*, **la sección del tiempo**, in a Mexican newspaper. Another guest takes a seat next to her and they start chatting about el tiempo.

82

Listen to the two women's conversation and give information in Spanish about the following.

1. the weather in la Ciudad de México

2. the weather in Argentina

3. where Harriet Herbert comes from

4. where the other woman comes from

5. Harriet's reason for being in la Ciudad de México

6. the other woman's reason for being in la Ciudad de México

Nuts & bolts
exchanging personal information

Saying where you're from:

¿De dónde es usted?	*Where are you from?*
Yo soy de Argentina.	*I am from ...*

Making introductions:

Henry, la señora/el señor ...	*Henry, this is Ms./Mrs./Mr. ...*
Yo soy Harriet, Harriet Herbert.	*I am ...*
Mucho gusto. (*moo*-cho *goos*-to)	*Pleased to meet you.*

Saying why you're travelling:

De vacaciones. (*de ba-ka-syo-nes*)	*On holiday.*
Por trabajo. (*por tra-ba-kho*)	*On business.*
	(literally: *For work.*)

⊚ 8₃

After a while, Harriet sees Henry come in. She calls him over and introduces him to her new acquaintance. Complete the conversation, then listen to it and practice taking Harriet's role.

Harriet:	**¡Ah! ¡Howard!**
Howard:	**Hola.**
Harriet:	**Howard, la señora ...**
Señora:	**Elena, Elena Varela.**

Harriet: _____ . **Mi esposo Howard, y**

_____ **Harriet, Harriet Herbert.**

Señora: _____

**go to
www.collinslanguage.com/revolution
for extra activities**

words to remember >>>

Las tiendas *(las **tyen**-das)*

The shops

Mind Map it!

Before learning some new words for food, make a Mind Map with all the words you already know for the sort of food you might buy in a market. Check you've remembered them all by looking back at Unidades 1, 3, and 6.

Green
FOR GO AHEAD

un kilo *(oon **kee**-lo)* a kilo

los gramos *(los **gra**-mos)* grams

un litro *(oon **lee**-tro)* a liter

los mangos *(los **man**-gos)* mangoes

los tomates *(los to-**ma**-tes)* tomatoes

el salmón *(el sal-**mon**)* salmon

una docena *(**oo**-na do-**the**-na)* a dozen

las sardinas *(las sar-**dee**-nas)* sardines

la lechuga *(la le-**choo**-ga)* lettuce

Remember to link these words with your strong male and female characters.

Yellow
FOR WAIT
AND THINK

el aceite de oliva
*(el a-**sey**-te de o-**lee**-ba)* olive oil

una barra de pan
*(oo-na **ba**-rra de pan)* a loaf of bread

las papas *(las **pah**-pas)* potatoes

la verdura *(la bair-**doo**-ra)* vegetables

la carnicería *(la kar-nee-se-**ree**-a)* the butcher's

la frutería *(la froo-te-**ree**-a)* the fruit store

la panadería *(la pa-na-de-**ree**-a)* the baker's

la pescadería
*(la pes-ka-de-**ree**-a)* the fish store

To remember the names of the shops, link them with the items they sell. For example, you buy **carne** at a **carnicería**.

Did you know?

Markets

Mexican people sometimes buy their food in covered or open-air markets, **mercados**, where there are food stalls of every kind. Local vendors bring regional specialties to market, so this is the place to come for some ingredients that you might not be able to find in a supermarket.

Shopping in a market is an entertaining experience and a good way to practice your Spanish, too!

Red
FOR STOP, THINK,
MAKE A LINK

 84

Listen to all
the words you
have seen
and practice
saying them.

el chorizo *(el cho-**ree**-so)* type of pork sausage

el salami *(el sal-la-mee)* salami

el azúcar *(el a-**soo**-kar)* sugar

los huevos *(los **we**-bos)* eggs

los plátanos *(los **pla**-ta-nos)* bananas

la tienda de abarrotes
*(la tien-da de a-ba-**rro**-tes)* the grocer's

la salchichonería
(la sal-she-sho-ne-ree-a) delicatessen, deli

la lata *(la **la**-ta)* tin

las fresas *(las **fre**-sas)* strawberries

las manzanas *(las man-**sa**-nas)* apples

las uvas *(las **oo**-bas)* grapes

las cebollas *(las se-**bo**-yas)* onions

Lata: "Put it in a tin to eat LATER!"

Plátanos: picture a fruit PLATTER with NO bananas!

Use your imagination to create images and associations
for the other words.

Mental gymnastics 5

Study the lists of red, green and yellow words, then turn the page and write as many as you can remember under each heading.

Fruta   **Verdura**   **Pescado**

....

....

....

....

....

Mental gymnastics 6

Match the items on the left with the tiendas where you can buy them.

1. sardinas   a. frutería

2. una barra de pan   b. carnicería

3. aceite de oliva   c. sachichonería

4. un bistec   d. panadería

5. atún   e. pescadería

6. naranjas   f. la tienda de abarrotes

Mental gymnastics 7

Match the quantities on the left with appropriate items on the right. Several combinations are possible.

un kilo		huevos
medio litro		atún
cien gramos		vino
una botella		pan
medio kilo		aceite
una docena	**de**	tomates
una barra		agua mineral
un litro		queso
dos latas		sardinas
un kilo y medio		pollo

Tony's Tip

The vocabulary tin

To test your vocabulary, set aside a tin and put in it all the words you need to know, written on pieces of paper or card: Spanish on one side and English on the other. Every day, pick 5 or 10 words out of the box. If you read the English side first, try to remember the Spanish, and vice versa.

If you get the word right, you can either put it back in the tin, to check you really do know it, or leave it out because you've learned it now. If you get it wrong, you must write the same word on another piece of paper and put both back in the tin. That way you double your chance of picking the word out next time!

How much is it?

Los señores Herbert say goodbye to the Argentinian lady and leave the hotel to pick up their hire car and set off for Guerrero.

And Guerrero is where the MacDonalds, *a Canadian family*, **una familia canadiense**, are spending their holidays in a village near Acapulco. They're in self-catering accommodation and el señor MacDonald, Alan, is getting ready to go to el mercado for food. He's making a Mind Map of everything he needs.

Nuts & bolts
asking the price

One item: **¿Cuánto cuesta una lechuga?**
How much does a lettuce cost?

More than one: **¿Cuánto cuestan cuatro naranjas?**
How much do four oranges cost?

One item: **¿A cuánto está el kilo de papas?**
How much is a kilo of potatoes?

More than one: **¿A cuánto están los tomates?**
How much are the tomatoes (per kilo)?

If you don't know the name of something, just point and ask: **¿Cuánto cuesta esto?** *How much does this cost?*

◎ 85

Read and listen to this short conversation between un tendero, *a shopkeeper*, and una clienta en el mercado. Then act it out, taking the part of la clienta in the pauses.

Tendero: **Buenos días. ¿Qué quería?**
Clienta: **¿A cuánto están las manzanas?**
Tendero: **Están a treinta pesos el kilo.**
Clienta: **Un kilo, por favor.**
Tendero: **¿Algo más?**
Clienta: **No, gracias.**

◎ 86

Now listen to Alan buying things in one of the shops in the market.

1. Tick the items he buys.

☐ dos litros de vino   ☐ un kilo de olivas

☐ un litro de aceite de oliva   ☐ un litro de agua mineral con gas

☐ una docena de huevos   ☐ una botella de vino tinto

☐ dos latas de atún

2. How much does he pay? ▭

3. Can you work out which shop he is in?

▭

Mental gymnastics 8

Read the "NUTS & BOLTS" on page 172, then complete these conversations and act them out.

1. **Hola. ¿Qué quería?**

    .... *How much are the potatoes?*
    Están a diez pesos el kilo.

    .... *Two kilos, please.*
    ¿Algo más?

    ....
    Yes, three lettuces, half a kilo of tomatoes, and a kilo of onions.

2. **Hola. ¿Qué quería?**

    ....
    100 grams of salami and 250 grams of cheese.
    Aquí tiene. ¿Algo más?

    .... *A bottle of water.*

3. **Buenos días. ¿Qué quería?**

    ....
    Three loaves of bread and a kilo of sugar.
    ¿Algo más?

    ....
    No, thanks. How much is it?
    Veintitres pesos.

87 Alan is now en la frutería buying some fruta. Listen to the conversation and complete the receipt.

Cantidad	Fruta	$
....	*fresas*	....
un kilo y cuarto de	....	....
....	....	....
....	....	....
....	....	....
	TOTAL:	....

88 Now it's your turn. You're going to la pescadería to buy some pescado. Complete the conversation, then listen and act it out.

Tendero: **Buenos días. ¿Qué quería?**

Usted:

Half a kilo of shrimp.

Tendero: **Aquí tiene. ¿Algo más?**

Usted:

Do you have salmon?

Tendero: **Sí, aquí. Es salmón canadiense.**

➤

Usted:	
How much is it per kilo?	
Tendero:	**A cien pesos.**
Usted:	
One kilo, please.	
Tendero:	**¿Algo más?**
Usted:	
No, thank you. How much is it?	
Tendero:	**Son doscientos setenta y cinco pesos.**

Mind Map it!

Add as many words as you can to the Mind Map.

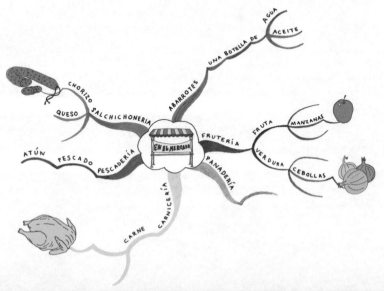

9

¡Soluciones!

By the end of this unit you will be able to:

- **Report missing luggage**
- **Talk to a doctor about your health**
- **Say that things don't work**
- **Ask if something can be repaired**

words to remember >>>

¿Cómo es? *(ko-mo es)*

What is it like?

el documento *(el do-koo-**men**-to)* document

Green
FOR GO AHEAD

el avión *(el a-**byon**)* airplane

el equipaje *(el e-kee-**pa**-khe)* luggage

la dirección *(la dee-rek-**syon**)* address

cuadrado, cuadrada
*(kwa-**dra**-do, kwa-**dra**-da)* square

Yellow
FOR WAIT
AND THINK

redondo, redonda *(re-**don**-do, re-**don**-da)* round

mañana *(ma-**nya**-na)* tomorrow

Avión is related to "aviation".

Equipaje is "equipment," but equipment for travelling.

For **dirección**, think of the "direction" you have to take to get to someone's address.

For **cuadrado**, picture a quadrangle that is square.

Redondo is similar to "rotund": round and plump.

You know that **mañana** means *morning*, so think of *tomorrow* as "in the morning."

Red

FOR STOP, THINK,
MAKE A LINK

 89

**Listen to the
green, yellow
and red words
and practice
saying them.**

una maleta *(oo-na ma-**le**-ta)* suitcase

una mochila *(oo-na mo-**chee**-la)* backpack

la etiqueta (de identificación)
*(la e-tee-**ke**-ta (de ee-den-tee-fee-ka-**syon**))* luggage label

el vuelo *(el **bwe**-lo)* flight

Here are suggested associations for two of these words.
Use your imagination to create your own.

For **maleta** imagine someone hitting a suitcase with a
wooden MALLET.

An **etiqueta** has nothing to do with etiquette or good
manners, but everything to do with putting a luggage
TICKET on a bag.

Nuts & bolts
describing things

What is it/are they like?
One thing: **¿Cómo es (la mochila)?**
More than one thing: **¿Cómo son (la maleta y la mochila)?**

It is .../They are ...
(La maleta) es grande/pequeña/mediana.
(La maleta y la mochila) son negras/
verdes/blancas.

Mental gymnastics 1

Read the four descriptions and match each one to an illustration.
Then write a description for the illustration that is left over.

a   b   c   d   e

1. .... Es pequeña y azul.

2. .... Es grande, cuadrada y roja.

3. .... Es redonda, mediana y naranja.

4. .... Es café y grande.

5. ....

check your answers at
www.collinslanguage.com/revolution

Mental gymnastics 2

Which of the following sentences refer to one missing item (1) and which refer to more than one (+)?

1/+

a. ☐ Falta una maleta.
b. ☐ Faltan una maleta y una mochila.
c. ☐ Falta una mochila.
d. ☐ Faltan una mochila y una maleta.

Underline the words that mean *is missing* or *are missing*. Can you see a pattern? Read the "NUTS & BOLTS" below to check.

Nuts & bolts
falta, faltan

Faltar is a verb (action word) meaning *to be missing*.
Falta and **faltan** are the forms of **faltar** that go with **maleta** and **maletas**.

One thing:
Falta una maleta.

More than one thing:
Faltan una maleta y una mochila.

Our luggage is missing!

La familia Smith — James, Caroline and their kids Megan and Josh — have just arrived al aeropuerto de Acapulco. They've rented **un apartamento** *an apartment* and can't wait to see it. But only one of their maletas is on the carousel; there's no sign of the second maleta or Josh's mochila. Caroline goes to **la oficina de reclamación de equipaje** *the baggage claim office* to report them missing.

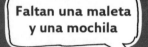

Faltan una maleta
y una mochila

90

Listen to Caroline talking to the employee and tick the correct information. Check your answers and then listen again and practice saying Caroline's lines along with her.

1. *Items missing:* Falta(n) ...
   a. ☐ una maleta
   b. ☐ una maleta y una mochila
   c. ☐ una mochila

2. *Documents requested:*
   a. ☐ el pasaporte
   b. ☐ el boleto
   c. ☐ las etiquetas del equipaje y el boleto

3. *The missing items are in:*
   a. ☐ Panamá
   b. ☐ Acapulco
   c. ☐ Ixtapa

4. La maleta es ...
   a. ▪ cuadrada y gris
   b. ▪ redonda y negra
   c. ▪ cuadrada y negra

5. La mochila es ...
   a. ▪ grande y verde
   b. ▪ grande y azul
   c. ▪ pequeña y verde

6. *Caroline's cell phone number:*
   a. ▪ 0763 59874
   b. ▪ 0765 39872
   c. ▪ 0755 39872

7. *The luggage will arrive:*
   a. ▪ mañana por la tarde
   b. ▪ mañana por la mañana
   c. ▪ esta tarde a las cuatro

8. *Phone number for information:*
   a. ▪ 415 678
   b. ▪ 415 768
   c. ▪ 514 815

Me siento mal *(me **syen**-to mal)*

I don't feel well

Green
FOR GO AHEAD

el estómago *(el es-**to**-ma-go)* stomach

los antibióticos *(los an-tee-**byo**-tee-kos)* antibiotics

el/la paciente *(el/la pa-**syen**-te)* patient

el médico *(el **me**-dee-ko)* doctor

la alergia *(la a-**lair**-kheea)* allergy

la aspirina *(la as-pee-**ree**-na)* aspirin

la fiebre *(la **fye**-bre)* fever

la indigestión *(la een-dee-khes-**tyon**)* indigestion

la infección *(la een-fek-**syon**)* infection

la penicilina *(la pe-nee-see-**lee**-na)* penicillin

Yellow
FOR WAIT
AND THINK

un catarro *(oon ka-**ta**-rro)* a cold

la receta *(la re-**se**-ta)* (medical) prescription

For **receta**, think of the RECEIPT you get when you pay for your medicine.

Red
FOR STOP, THINK,
MAKE A LINK

 91

Listen to the green, yellow and red words and practice saying them.

el dolor *(el do-**lor**)* ache, pain

el jarabe *(el kha-**ra**-be)* (cough) syrup

la cabeza *(la ka-**be**-sa)* head

la garganta *(la gar-**gan**-ta)* throat

la gripa *(la **gree**-pa)* flu

una insolación *(**oo**-na een-so-la-**syon**)* sunstroke

la tos *(la tos)* cough

Here are our associations for some of these words. When you create your own, remember to link the nouns with your super-masculine or super-feminine character.

Gripa: when they have the flu, some people GRIPE and complain about it.

Insolación: you need INSULATION from the sun if you get sunstroke.

For **tos**, imagine Doña Maria playing cards: she coughs violently and TOSSes the cards ino the air.

Mind Map it!

Study the Mind Map "At the doctor's".

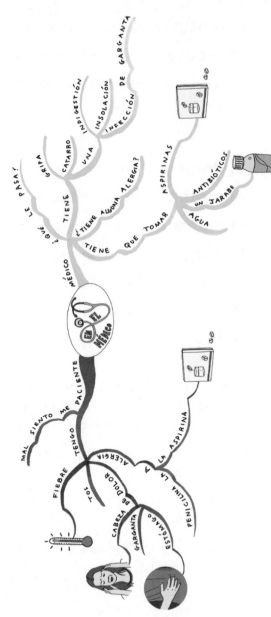

Cover up our Mind Map and draw your own. Then check: did you remember everything?

At the doctor's

The missing equipaje has arrived and la familia Smith is really enjoying the holiday. But one morning Caroline gets up feeling unwell: **se siente mal**. She decides to see un médico.

92

Listen to two conversations between un médico and los pacientes and write the number of the conversation next to each piece of information you hear.

Problema	Diagnóstico	Tratamiento
☐ dolor de cabeza	☐ gripa	☐ jarabe
☐ fiebre	☐ insolación	☐ agua
☐ tos	☐ indigestión	☐ antibióticos
☐ dolor de estómago	☐ infección de garganta	☐ sol
☐ dolor de garganta	☐ catarro	☐ aspirinas

Mental gymnastics 3

Cover up the Mind Map and match the pictures with the phrases.

a   b   c   d   e

1. Tengo dolor de estómago. 2. Tengo fiebre. 3. Tengo tos.
4. Tengo dolor de cabeza. 5. Tengo dolor de garganta.

93 Listen to Caroline's conversation with the doctor and fill in the details. Then practice saying Caroline's lines along with her.

Caroline's symptoms: Tengo

Doctor's diagnosis: Tiene

Caroline's allergies: Tengo

Doctor's prescription: Tiene que tomar

Caroline comes home with la receta and James takes it to **la farmacia** *the drug store.*

 94 Listen to James's conversation with **la farmacéutica** *the pharmacist.* What is James buying? How much does it cost?

95 Now it's your turn. You have a prescription for penicillin and you also need a cough syrup. Listen and act out the conversation with el farmacéutico.

Did you know?

Buying medicines in Mexico

If you decide to buy prescription drugs in Mexico, ask your US pharmacist to provide you with a tiny brochure called a "package insert" that is attached to all bottles of US wholesale medicines. This insert has exactly the same information listed in a huge reference book called *Physicians Desk Reference* (or PDR). The package insert contains an enormous amount of information about the medicine, including its generic name, dosage formulations and other information.

go to
www.collinslanguage.com/revolution
for extra activities

words to remember >>>

Necesito ... *(ne-se-**see**-to)*

I need ...

Green
FOR GO AHEAD

Yellow
FOR WAIT
AND THINK

un mecánico *(oon me-**ka**-nee-ko)* mechanic

un plomero *(oon plo-**meh**-ro)* plumber

un técnico *(oon **tek**-nee-ko)* technician

el refrigerador *(el re-free-hea-ra-**dor**)* refrigerator

reparar *(re-pa-**rar**)* to repair

el auto *(el **aw**-to)* car

no funciona *(no foon-**syo**-na)* it doesn't work

Here are some suggestions for remembering the yellow words.

For **auto**, think of the word "automobile".

Think of **funciona** as "it functions".

Red
FOR STOP, THINK,
MAKE A LINK

la lavadora *(la la-ba-**do**-ra)* washing machine

la estufa *(la es-**too**-fa)* stove

la regadera *(la re-ga-**deh**-ra)* shower

⊙ **96**

**Listen to the
green, yellow
and red words
and practice
saying them.**

Create images to help you remember these new words:
the more bizarre, the better! For example, imagine a LAB
where DORA, up to her elbows in soap suds, is trying to
mend a broken **lavadora**.

Mental gymnastics 4

Write what doesn't work in each picture and who you need to make
it work again.

1 2 3 4 5

1. *El refrigerador no funciona. Necesito un técnico.*

2. ....

3. ....

4. ....

5. ....

It doesn't work!

La familia Smith has rented un auto and set off for a day at the Parque Papagayo theme park. Suddenly el auto starts making a strange noise. They stop to look at the engine and it won't start again. Luckily, una mujer is passing and she asks **"¿Qué le pasa? ¿Tiene un problema?"** *What's the matter? Do you have a problem?*

 97

Listen to James's conversations with la mujer and un mecánico. Answer the questions in English. Then read the transcript and practice saying James's lines along with him.

1. James doesn't understand the woman at first. What does he ask her to do?

2. Where can he find a mechanic?

3. How long does the mechanic need to repair the car?

Tony's Tip

Be curious!

Be totally curious about *everything* to do with your new language: keep your eyes and your ears wide open for *anything* to do with your new language. Your teacher should be *everyone* you meet who speaks your new language!

Mental gymnastics 5

Now it's your turn. The shower in your apartment doesn't work, so you call on your Mexican **vecina**, neighbour, to see if she can help. Complete the conversations.

1. Vecina mexicana: **Hola, buenos días.**

    Usted: ....

    I have a problem. The shower doesn't work.

    Vecina mexicana: **Ah, hay un plomero cerca de aquí.**

    Usted: ....

    Can you repeat, please? I don't understand.

    Vecina mexicana: **Un plomero, para reparar la regadera.**

    Usted: ....

    ¡Ah! A plumber. Where?

    Vecina mexicana: **Cerca, aquí tiene usted la dirección.**

    Usted: ....

    Thank you.

2. Plomero: **Buenos días. ¿En qué puedo ayudarle?**

    Usted: *¿Puede* ....

    Can you repair a shower?

    Plomero: **Sí, puedo repararla.**

    Usted: ....

    When?

    Plomero: **Hmm ... Esta tarde.**

    Usted: ....

    OK, thank you.

use CD2
for more audio practice and revision

10

¡Hasta la vista!

Now you can:

- Speak and understand Spanish well enough to feel confident and relaxed when travelling around, asking for information, shopping, and using services

- Understand information in Spanish about the places you're planning to visit

Congratulations! You've reached the final unit of your course! It's a revision unit where you get the chance to practice and consolidate the language you've learned. If you've forgotten a word or phrase you need for an exercise, just go back to the relevant unit and revise it. Remember Tony's tip:

Five times repetition = long-term memory!

Making sure you understand

Mental gymnastics 1

<<< Unidad 4
Unidad 8

What you would say in the following situations?

1. You don't understand what la dependienta en una tienda is saying.

   ....

2. The employee en la oficina de turismo assumes you speak Spanish really well.

   ....

3. El recepcionista en el hotel is speaking too fast.

   ....

4. You are en una tienda and you don't know what **cinturón** means.

   ....

5. La mujer sitting next to you en el tren says something you don't understand, so you'd like her to repeat it.

   ....

Introducing yourself

Mental gymnastics 2   <<< Unidad 8

Give yourself 60 seconds to write these phrases in Spanish.

1. Where are you from?   ....
2. I'm from the US/Canada/England.   ....
3. And you?   ....
4. I'm from Mexico/France/Wales.   ....
5. I'm (name).   ....
6. Pleased to meet you.   ....

<<< Unidad 2

Accommodation

You are checking into a hotel. You've booked a single room with bathroom, for one night. Listen to the conversation on track 25 and act it out. After the receptionist speaks, there's a pause for you to answer and then you'll hear the correct answer.

Using public transport

98

<<< Unidad 7

Look at the departure time for the bus from la Ciudad de México to Toluca. Write down how to ask in Spanish "At what time does the bus to Toluca leave?" Then listen and check the three answers you hear.

a. ■ 5:15   e. ■ 18:40

b. ■ 9:20   f. ■ 21:10

c. ■ 13:00   g. ■ 23:05

d. ■ 15:30

Mental gymnastics 3   <<< Unidad 7

Write down how you would ask for the following tickets.

1. A one-way ticket to Mérida.   ....

2. Two one-way tickets to Cancún.   ....

3. A round-trip ticket to Ixtapa.   ....

Mental gymnastics 4 <<< Unidad 7

Complete the conversation at the bus station and then practice it aloud.

Boletero: **Buenas tardes.**

Usted: ....
Good afternoon. What time are there buses to Cuernavaca?

Boletero: **Cada veinte minutos. Hay uno a las cuatro y diez de la tarde.**

Usted: ....
What time does it arrive?

Boletero: **Llega a las cinco y veinte.**

Usted: ....
How much does a round-trip ticket cost?

Boletero: **Cincuenta pesos.**

Usted: ....
Two round-trip tickets, please.

Boletero: **Aquí tiene, son cien pesos.**

Tony's Tip

Use your Spanish!

Don't be shy about speaking Spanish! It doesn't matter if you make mistakes: even native speakers make them. The only way to learn is by practicing, and people will appreciate your efforts. So take every opportunity to use your Spanish: talk and listen to Spanish speakers, watch films and TV programs in Spanish, read magazines, leaflets, newspapers, and websites in Spanish — and, most of all, have fun!

Mental gymnastics 5

<<< Unidad 2

You're in a taxi. Say where you want to go.

1. ¿Adónde va usted?

....
to the airport

2. ¿Adónde va usted?

....
to the train station

3. ¿Adónde van ustedes?

....
to the Hotel Miramar

Asking the way

Mental gymnastics 6

<<< Unidad 3
Unidad 5

You want to know IF THERE IS one of these places nearby. What do you ask?

1. una oficina de turismo
2. una estación de autobuses
3. una farmacia
4. un restaurante

You want to know WHERE each of these is. What do you ask?

5. el museo Frida Kahlo
6. el Hotel Río
7. la estación de tren
8. los probadores

Mental gymnastics 7

<<< Unidad 3
Unidad 5

Look at the map and complete the conversation.

– ¿Dónde .... la estación de autobuses?

– Saliendo del hotel, ...

Eating out

Mind Map it!

<<< Unidad 1
Unidad 3
Unidad 6

Take a blank piece of paper and some colored
pens and make a Mind Map using all the food and drink
words you know.

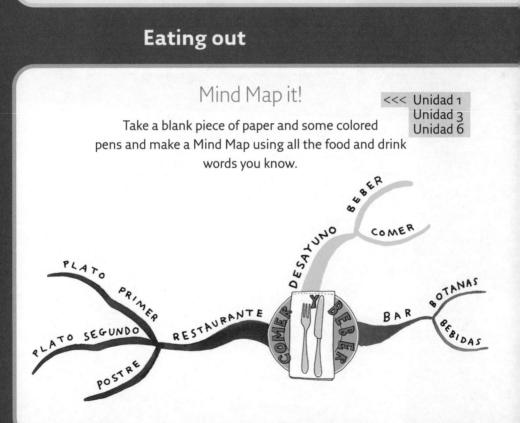

99

<<< Unidad 8

Read la carta del restaurante El Rosal. Listen to the two conversations and fill in the table.

	Conversación 1	Conversación 2
Primer plato		
Segundo plato		
Bebida		
Postre		
La cuenta		

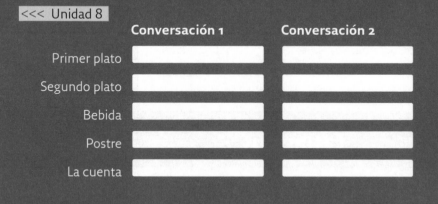

Restaurante El Rosal

Entrantes
Camarones fritos — $100
Ensalada mixta — $80
Ensalada verde — $80

Sopas
Sopa de pescado — $115
Sopa de verduras — $100

Carnes
Bistec de ternera — $200
Pollo al tequila — $150

Pescados
Salmón a la mexicana — $180
Atún a la plancha — $180

Postres
Flan de la casa — $60
Mousse de queso — $50
Mousse de chocolate — $40
Nieve — $60

El restaurante cierra la noche del domingo y el lunes todo el día.

Shopping

Mental gymnastics 8 <<< Unidad 5

In 30 seconds, match the illustrations with the descriptions.

1 2

3 4

a. un suéter rojo
b. una falda negra
c. una camisa amarilla
d. un pantalón café

Mental gymnastics 9 <<< Unidad 5
Unidad 7

Act out the conversation. Then replace **el suéter** with **la camisa**, remembering to make the other changes you need to go with a feminine noun.

Dependienta: **¿ En qué puedo ayudarle?**
Cliente: **El suéter me queda pequeño.**
¿Lo tienen en la talla mediana?
Dependienta: **Un momento, por favor. ... Sí, aquí tiene.**
Cliente: **Gracias.**

...

Cliente: **El suéter me queda bien. Me lo llevo.**

Mental gymnastics 10

<<< Unidad 5
Unidad 7

Use the phrases below to complete the conversation in the department store.

– *Aquí tiene.*
– *En blanco, por favor.*
– *Por favor, ¿cuánto cuesta este sombrero?*
– *Gracias y adiós.*
– *En efectivo.*
– *¿En qué colores lo tienen?*

Clienta: ....

Dependiente: **Quinientos pesos.**

Clienta: ....

Dependiente: **En blanco, en negro y en rojo.**

Clienta: ....

Dependiente: **¿Cómo quiere pagar usted: con tarjeta de crédito o en efectivo?**

Clienta: ....

Dependiente: **Muy bien. Son quinientos pesos.**

Clienta: ....

Dependiente: **Muchas gracias. Adiós.**

Clienta: ....

Mental gymnastics 11 <<< Unidad 7

Look at the illustrations and say whether you like or dislike the clothes, according to the symbols.

1. ....

2. ....

3. ....

4. ....

5. ....

Mind Map it! <<< Unidad 8

Draw a Mind Map for buying food en el mercado. Your main branches are FRUTERÍA, CARNICERÍA, SACHICHONERÍA, PANADERÍA, PESCADERÍA, TIENDA DE ABARROTES. Compare your new Mind Map with the one you drew for Unit 8. Did you remember everything?

Mental gymnastics 12

<<< Unidad 8

Complete the conversations and then act them out.

1. **Buenos días. ¿Qué quería?**

.... *How much is a kilo of oranges?*

A treinta pesos.

.... *A kilo and a half, please.*

¿Algo más?

.... *No, thanks.*

2. **Hola. ¿Qué quería?**

.... *How much are the sardines?*

Están a ciento veinte pesos el kilo.

.... *One kilo, please.*

¿Algo más?

.... *Yes, half a kilo of shrimp.*

3. **Hola. ¿Qué quería?**

....

A kilo of sugar and 200 grams of cheese.
¿Algo más?

.... *A bottle of water.*

The weather

Mental gymnastics 13

<<< Unidad 8

Describe the weather in these cities and react to it, as in the example.

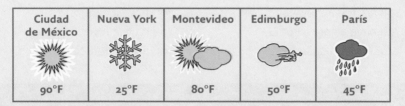

Ciudad de México	Nueva York	Montevideo	Edimburgo	París
90°F	25°F	80°F	50°F	45°F

En la Ciudad de México hace buen tiempo: hace sol y hace calor.
Hace noventa. ¡Qué calor!

Mind Map it!

Complete the Mind Map for "El tiempo."
Compare your new Mind Map with the
one you drew for Unit 8. Is it the same?

<<< Unidad 8

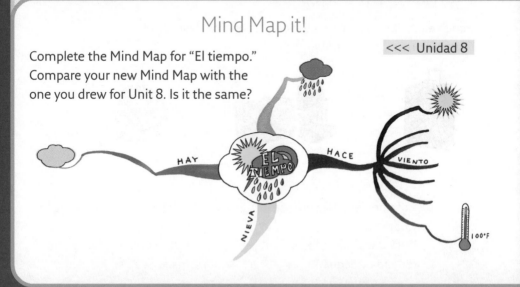

At the doctor's

Mental gymnastics 14 <<< Unidad 9

What would you say to un médico in the following situations?

1. You are feeling unwell.
2. You have a sore throat.
3. You have a headache.
4. You have a cough.
5. You have a fever.
6. You are allergic to penicillin.

Solving problems

Mental gymnastics 15 <<< Unidad 9

Match each illustration with the corresponding description.
(There is one extra description.)

a

b

c

1. .... Falta una mochila grande y naranja.
2. .... Falta una maleta rosa, redonda y pequeña.
3. .... Falta una maleta cuadrada y verde.
4. .... Faltan una mochila y una maleta cafés.